THE LUTHERAN VENTURE
IN
HIGHER EDUCATION

THE KNUBEL-MILLER LECTURES FOR 1962

The
Lutheran Venture
in
Higher Education

By

Gould Wickey

Board of Publication of the United Lutheran Church in America

Philadelphia

DEDICATED

to my wife, *Ethel,*

and

to our daughters, *Kathryn, Phyllis, Vivian,* and *Charlotte,*
all of whom experienced a blessing from
the Lutheran venture in higher education

ACKNOWLEDGMENTS

The author wishes to thank: (*a*) the publishers of various books and magazines for permission to use certain quotations in the text of this volume; (*b*) the offices of the Commission on College and University Work of The Lutheran Church-Missouri Synod and of the Division of College and University Work of the National Lutheran Council, the presidents of Lutheran colleges and seminaries, and a number of campus pastors for providing valued information not otherwise available; and (*c*) the Board of Higher Education of the United Lutheran Church in America for the privilege of being a Knubel-Miller lecturer.

TABLE OF CONTENTS

"The right instruction of youth is a matter in which Christ and all the world are concerned. . . . It is indeed a sin and shame that we must be aroused and incited to the duty of educating our children and of considering their highest interests. . . . And what would it avail if we possessed all else, and became perfect saints, if we neglect that for which we chiefly live, namely, to care for the young? In my judgment, there is no other outward offense that in the sight of God so heavily burdens the world, and deserves such heavy chastisement, as the neglect to educate children."—*From Luther's letter to the mayors and aldermen of all the cities of Germany in behalf of Christian schools.*

PREFACE

It was a significant experience in the life of a Lutheran student when he walked through a Harvard gate on a September day in 1915 and saw the motto *Veritas Pro Christo et Ecclesia.* That motto has been his guide during the intervening years. Here was his inspiration for a Christian ecumenicity in the field of higher education.

On a September day in 1920 that same Lutheran walked on the campus of a small (at that time) Lutheran college in Minnesota to serve as a professor of philosophy. (Concordia College has no gates.) Since that year he has walked on the campuses of all, except a couple, Lutheran colleges and seminaries, and of scores of non-Lutheran colleges, universities, and seminaries. These were not merely casual "walks"; most of them were opportunities to study and observe, and a sizable number were to survey and evaluate. Visits to the campuses of non-Lutheran universities gave him opportunities to observe the Lutheran church at work in the campus ministry.

The very title of these lectures enables the lecturer to draw upon his experiences, observations, and studies during a period of some forty years. So the purpose is to bring together certain historical and current facts, some of which are not easily gathered and not generally known, concerning higher education in all Lutheran bodies in America, then to examine policies and programs, and, finally, to indicate some problems and possibilities which need consideration as the Lutheran church faces a changing future.

The purpose in establishing this lectureship was to "furnish fresh, inspiring, and practical lectures to pastors of the church in active charge of congregations." The lectures in this 1962 series may be "fresh" in their presentation of higher education for all the Lutheran bodies in America, which has never been done before, "informing" by bringing together some of the latest data and information on Lutheran higher education, and "practical" in the suggestion of possibilities for developments in the years ahead. Whether they are "inspiring" depends upon the skill of the author in communicating the facts and his analysis of problems and possibilities, as well as the interest and receptivity of the readers and the awakened decisions to solve current problems and to grasp the prospect for a larger and more effective program of higher education in the Lutheran church.

It will become quite clear to the reader that each chapter might well be expanded into a volume. In fact, the author hopes that in the not too distant future historically minded educators, collegiate and theological, may be inspired and officially encouraged and supported in making such contributions to the literature of higher education in the Lutheran church. Education is one of the most vital issues before the church, but many within the church have not yet come to realize that fact.

In this volume pastors and laymen will have available a comprehensive, although telescopic, view of the Lutheran church's program of higher education, and may obtain a clearer understanding of some problems, which may stimulate a determination to encourage and, perhaps, to participate in the development of a program of Lutheran higher education with even higher-quality standards than exist at present. If such experiences be stimulated by these lectures, then a labor of love will not have been in vain.

GOULD WICKEY

APRIL, 1962
WASHINGTON, D.C.

I

WHY THE VENTURE?

Bewilderment, confusion, and despair are terms frequently used to characterize our present age. As these lectures are being written in the latter part of 1961, the conditions in international relationships make those words more realistic than ever. World Wars I and II have reaffirmed the testimony of history that wars never settle international problems permanently. Even science is no longer conceived to be "an avalanche which will cleanse the world," as H. G. Wells once thought, and then before his death indicated an attitude of utter despair. In fact, science has given man the power to blow up our planet and to destroy mankind with all his powers. This atomic power ought to force "mankind into a greater humanity," as Arthur H. Compton declared, but the "ought" has not yet become "is." This is part of the reason why someone has spoken of the history of the first half of the twentieth century as "a history of deepening horror."[1]

Education is not free from the condition of confusion. W. H. Kilpatrick wrote in *The Educational Frontier:* "There probably never was a time during the past century when the American people were less sure of the essential finality of their institutions than they are at the present moment. But what is it that is wrong? On this point we seem to be pretty much at sea. For this situation education, owing to its own inherent confusion, must accept a large measure of responsibility."[2]

[1] See Howard Mumford Jones, *Education and World Tragedy* (Cambridge: Harvard University Press, 1946), pp. 3-9.
[2] W. H. Kilpatrick, *The Educational Frontier* (New York: D. Appleton-Century Co., 1933), p. 6.

1

What was written three decades ago is applicable to education in 1962. As a result, through the years education has been subject to severe criticism. To clarify the educational atmosphere, colleges and seminaries have been engaged in self-surveys and evaluations, or in such surveys and evaluations as may be conducted by well-trained and experienced educators.

Under such conditions it is quite proper to inquire why the Lutheran church entered into the field of higher education, even though the conditions at the beginning of the nineteenth century may not have been identical with those of the twentieth century. The Lutheran church had no past in America to perpetuate. The answer may easily be given: the Lutheran church needed a ministry trained on the field, for the field, by the field, with no dependence on ministers trained in Europe. This answer is equally applicable to all Lutheran bodies. While this need did exist, the answer does not account for the whole program of higher education in the Lutheran church. So these questions still persist in raising their heads: Why have new Lutheran colleges been established in countries (Canada and the United States) where there already exist hundreds of non-Lutheran schools able to educate the youth of our church? Why are millions of dollars being spent on a ministry to Lutheran students and faculty members on the campuses of non-Lutheran educational institutions?

In this decade of the twentieth century some good but not necessarily basic answers may be given to these questions. It may be said that the large bulge of students seeking admission to colleges cannot be cared for by the nonchurch institutions. This assumes that the church has a definite educational policy and that its funds cannot be used better elsewhere. Again, it may be answered that the church has already invested large sums in its schools, in facilities and endowments, which should be protected. But this assumes that the church's program of higher education is worth protecting. Further, it may be said, students and faculty members in a large university are mere numbers and lose their identity, while in the smaller church schools they are recognized as persons. To a degree this may be true, but some Lutheran schools will soon be as large as Harvard University was fifty years ago. Finally, it may be said and it has been said that the church needs to continue and even increase its program of higher education in order to act as a bulwark "against threats to intellectual and academic freedom stemming from economic, political, and social forces within our culture." This is true but only on the assumption that the church itself allows academic freedom and that the church is strong enough to stem the tide of nonreligious and non-Christian forces in our present-day culture.

So the questions persist: Why is the church, the Lutheran church, in the field of higher education? or, why has the church developed a program of higher education within, or alongside of, its evangelistic program and responsibility? Just why did the Lutheran church venture in higher education? Is there a Lutheran philosophy of education? If so, what is it?

THE PROBLEM OF A PHILOSOPHY OF LUTHERAN EDUCATION

Before attempting to discuss this problem, it is necessary that certain terms be defined. Education has been defined by many persons, in many ways, and from various points of view, such as the goal, the purpose, the method, the student, the subject-matter, and the teacher. To record several of these would lead only to confusion. I would merely say that education is the complete and harmonious development of all the powers (capacities) of an individual, through observation, information, instruction, inspiration, revelation, and activation, for his own welfare, in the interest of mankind, and to the glory and service of God. This definition is meant to include formal and informal education. The capacities of an individual include the physical, intellectual, social, aesthetic, moral, and spiritual. Education is not an end in itself; its use is for the individual, mankind, and God. This definition is quite different from that of the idealist, who conceives of education as essentially "intellectual apprehension and contemplation." It is different from that of the naturalist, who thinks of education primarily as a matter of "stimulus and response," or of changing the environment. Our definition of education requires a *development* and *commitment* of the whole person in time, in this life, to ends beyond himself and yet with which he is intimately related. It is admitted that such development and commitment is not completed or perfected in this life, at least so far as I have been able to discern. Natural man is subject to conditions and powers which tend to prevent him from attaining his highest goals. But this is no reason why man in his educational program should not set up the highest objectives. We never hit higher than we aim; it is generally lower, at least in the realm of the moral and the spiritual.

Lutheran education is not an education by Lutherans and for Lutherans. The number of Lutheran students, the number of Lutheran faculty members, and even the ownership of a school by the Lutheran church do not guarantee a Lutheran education. *Lutheran education is an education permeated by the thought and life of the Lutheran church.*

The word "philosophy" means "the love of wisdom." As interpreted by Greek philosophers, it means "the search for wisdom." German philosophers have used the compound word *"Weltanschauung,"* meaning "world view," as the goal of the philosopher's search. So Weber defines philosophy as "the search for a comprehensive view of nature, an attempt at a universal explanation of things."[3] It should be noted that actually the search for the first cause is really ontology or metaphysics, which, then,

[3] Alfred Weber, *History of Philosophy* trans. by Frank Thilly (New York: Charles Scribner's Sons, 1912), p. 1.

is only a part of philosophy. A philosophy of education would include a consideration of the whole field of education: its history, principles, levels, programs, and product. So we can say a philosophy of education is "the application of fundamental principles of life to the work of education. These principles guide indispensably or ought to guide educational theory and practice, aims and objectives, content and methods, educational psychology, teacher training, administration and research."[4]

In recent years there has been expression of the idea that we ought to speak of the theology of education. What is *theology?* Theology is man's systematic arrangement of the doctrines found in the Bible, which is considered to be in a distinct sense God's revelation to man. Note that the emphasis is on man's arrangement of the doctrines. Sometimes there seems to be the opinion that theology as such is as sacred as the Bible itself, that theology is the "mouthpiece" of God. This is not so. As the work of man, theology is never absolutely fixed. The discovery of new manuscripts, the new translations, and the more correct interpretations in light of new knowledge will lead to a new, or better, formulation of the doctrines of theology. A theology of education would be and is a presentation of the theological principles on which an educational system is based. But this is not a philosophy of education; it is only a part of a philosophy of education.

Can There Be a Lutheran Philosophy of Education?

Some Lutheran educators bemoan the fact that there is no commonly accepted Lutheran philosophy of education which directs the program of Lutheran education. Then come some Lutheran theologians who claim that there can be no Lutheran philosophy of education. They say, in essence, that philosophy is a reasoning, a thinking, a world view, and that there is no particular or pe-

[4] Redden and Ryan, *A Catholic Philosophy of Education* (Milwaukee: The Bruce Publishing Company, 1956, rev. ed.), p. 10.

culiar way in which Lutherans think. When Lutherans think, they must think according to the laws of sound reasoning. So Lutheran thinking cannot be different from the thinking of other people. Further, these theologians argue that Lutherans in their educational programs include ideas established on the basis of revelation, and revelation is outside the realm of reasoning, and therefore beyond philosophy. Theologians who argue thus have an inadequate conception of philosophy.

Philosophy tries to weave into a systematic whole all that is. If revelation is a reality—and I believe it is—then philosophy must bring it into the whole system presented. The method of revelation may be beyond the powers of human reasoning, but that does not invalidate the facts related to revelation. Somehow revelation and inspiration must be accepted, even though rationally they may not be understood in 1962. Much of the accomplishments of science in the twentieth century would probably have been denied as impossible by scientists of the first century. So philosophers may not be able to explain certain experiences, but they cannot deny the facts of the experience.

In spite of the attitude of some theologians, there are books which claim to be Christian philosophies of education. Volumes which are of considerable value have been prepared by individuals or groups within certain Christian groups. For the Catholics there appeared in 1956 from the pens of Redden and Ryan the volume entitled *A Catholic Philosophy of Education*. This book is extensively used in Catholic colleges. However, a prominent professor in a Catholic university told this writer that there is no one volume which would be considered the official statement of the Catholic philosophy of education. Under Presbyterian auspices a conference was held at Jamestown College, North Dakota, which resulted in the book *Toward a Christian Philosophy of Higher Education*. Of the eleven addresses printed in this volume, three are by Lutheran educators. A Lutheran volume, *Christian Faith*

and the Liberal Arts, published in 1960, has seventeen chapters
by fifteen authors, representing essentially one Lutheran body.
They agree on certain fundamental religious and intellectual
points, but frankly admit that they do not set forth a distinctively
"Lutheran" position. Their point of view is, they say, "broadly
representative of the classical intellectual tradition of the Western
church, qualified in important ways by Reformation concerns."
The Board of Parish Education of The Lutheran Church-Missouri
Synod has appointed a committee to make "a thorough systematic
study of Lutheran principles of education," which essentially will
be a Lutheran philosophy of education; but the results of their
study have not yet (1962) been published. However, Allan H.
Jahsmann, a member of this Committee on the Lutheran Philosophy of Education, has already published *What's Lutheran in
Education?* This work, he claims, is "not an official statement of
the Lutheran philosophy of education," but it is "a personal study
of what Lutheran theologians and educators have thought about
basic concerns in a philosophy of education. . . . It is only pre-
liminary to the integrated statement of Lutheran educational
theory so urgently needed." As to whether there is a Lutheran
philosophy of education, Dr. Jahsmann answers: "In the measure
that theology determines a person's point of view, to that extent
it is a part of his philosophy. And when a Lutheran applies
Lutheran theology to the questions of education or systematizes
his educational thinking in harmony with his theological principles, to that extent his theology is the basis of his educational
philosophy, the foundations on which he builds his structure of
thinking."[5]

I agree with the truth of Jahsmann's position, but I believe it
is better to speak of a philosophy of Lutheran education which
will include all the "principles, factors, qualities and characteristics that are essential to Lutheranism and typical of anything

[5] A. H. Jahsmann, *What's Lutheran in Education?* (St. Louis: Concordia Publishing House, 1960), p. x.

classifiable as Lutheran." I cannot escape the fact that Lutheran thinking must be in harmony with sound logical thinking, but the difference lies not in *how* Lutherans think but *about what* they think, what they include in their total educational principles and programs. The adjective "Lutheran" should modify the word "education," rather than the word "philosophy." So a philosophy of Lutheran education will include: (1) a Lutheran theology with its Biblical principles; (2) an epistemology which recognizes the reality of revelation, inspiration, reasoning, and observation as channels of knowledge; (3) an ontology which recognizes the reality of a personal God in the universe, who revealed himself supremely in the person of Jesus Christ; (4) a psychology which admits the reality of spirit in persons and the effect of the Holy Spirit in the lives of persons; (5) a sociology which recognizes the worth of all persons in all human relations; (6) a pedagogy which accepts the best laws of learning formulated by man and the power of the Holy Spirit in achieving man's highest development; and (7) an axiology which sets up the glory of God and the welfare of man as the ultimate goals and values in education. Such a philosophy of Lutheran education will give consideration to the scope of the educational program, the content and organization of the curriculum, the effective methods of instruction, the efficiency of the teachers, the student needs and differences, the organization, support, and administration of the educational system, and the agencies involved.

In 1948 the Lutheran Theological Study Group produced a paper on "The Lutheran Church and Education," in which are set forth the theological foundation, the principles of education based on this foundation, and the resulting program of education, with some of the problems involved. The paper was never printed, but it was distributed in mimeographed form to a group of laymen interested in the subject. While it was primarily an outline, it does show that a theology of Lutheran education is possible and that Lutheran educators from nine Lutheran bodies can agree on a theology of Lutheran education.[6]

To present a complete philosophy of Lutheran education would require a sizable volume, written perhaps by a group of Lutheran educators with theological insight and educational knowledge and experience. So what is presented here in one lecture can be only a simple summary or outline of what may be considered by some as primarily a theology of education. However, what follows in this chapter, as well as in the other chapters, does have significance within a philosophy of Lutheran higher education.

TOWARD A THEOLOGY OF LUTHERAN EDUCATION

Naturally, in outline form this presentation will appear incomplete, but most of the basic ideas and principles will be included. Other educators might be inclined to give some different emphases and applications; however, what follows will give a broad insight into what is involved in this whole problem.

Biblical Foundation

1. The Bible is the source of religious knowledge and truth, wherein God's nature, purpose, and will are revealed (Rom. 1:16; 10:17; II Pet. 1:21).

2. God is personal and triune, three persons in one divine essence, Father, Son, and Holy Spirit (Rom. 1:2-4).

3. God created all things—heaven, earth, all creatures, and man—and that which he created was "very good" (Gen., chs. 1, 2; Rev. 4:11).

[6] President O. P. Kretzmann, of Valparaiso University, and the author of these lectures were the coauthors of the paper. After severe criticism by the group and a rewriting of certain sections by T. A. Kantonen, of Hamma Divinity School, the paper was distributed to some laymen. The writer is indebted to the discussion of this group for some of the direction of his own thinking in this chapter.

4. God created man in his own image, as body and soul, and for his fellowship. Thus the nature and purpose of man is found beyond man. Being endowed with reason, emotion, and will, man finds his full realization in mutual companionship with his fellow man and in fellowship with God. Since man has been created in the image of God, his original state appears to be one of perfection and immortality.

5. Man, by disobedience to his Creator's will, fell from his original state of perfection and became subject to sin. Because of this disobedience man is at enmity with God and under his condemnation (Gen. 3:14-19).

6. The God of love provided a way of reconciliation through the revelation of himself in Jesus Christ and man's acceptance of Jesus Christ as his Saviour. This is where God reveals his forgiving love through Jesus Christ as man's Saviour. It is the gospel, the "good news," the eternal Word of God (Rom. 3:21-28), and it is central in any Lutheran program of education; all else is peripheral.

7. Man appropriates God's forgiveness of sins through his personal faith in Jesus Christ as the divine Saviour from sin.

8. In the fallen state man cannot believe unless the power to believe is given through the Holy Spirit operating in and through the Word of God, producing repentance and faith in Christ.

9. Putting on the image of God or becoming perfect (Matt. 5:48) is a process from birth and is the continued goal of the Christian.

10. Man experiencing forgiveness also experiences a release from the impediments of this life. Man develops a new sense of values and judges all things in the light of God's will: he has a new perspective.

11. All such believers in the gospel constitute the true church, the body of Christ, of which he is the head (Eph. 1:22).

Lutheran Theological Principles

Luther summarized the Biblical principles in four phrases which have significance in a theology of Lutheran education:

1. *Sola Scriptura*—the supremacy and authoritativeness of Scripture or God's Word. Luther and the Lutheran church do not intend by this principle to set up the Bible as an external authority to rival the Roman pope. The Word as "the gospel of God concerning his Son" validates itself as a means of divine grace and regenerator of personalities. It proves itself to be inspired of God by being "profitable for teaching, for reproof, for correction, and for training in righteousness, that the man of God may be complete, equipped for every good work" (II Tim. 3:16, 17).

It is in these Scriptures that the Lutheran church finds its mandate to develop an educational program, especially in the last command of Jesus when he said: "All authority in heaven and on earth has been given to me. Go therefore and make disciples of all nations, baptizing them in the name of the Father and of the Son and of the Holy Spirit, teaching them to observe all that I have commanded you; and lo, I am with you always, to the close of the age" (Matt. 28:18-20).

Likewise, Paul wrote to the Colossians concerning this eternal gospel, "Him we proclaim, warning every man and teaching every man in all wisdom, that we may present every man mature in Christ" (Col. 1:28).

2. *Solus Christus*—Christ alone. Christ is the revelation of God and through him man finds his return to God.

3. *Sola Gratia*—justification by grace. Man finds his justification through the love of God and in this undeserved love all men become one in Christ Jesus.

4. *Sola Fides*—faith alone. Man is restored to a right relationship to God and to his fellow men through faith in God's

forgiving love manifested in Jesus Christ. From this principle comes that famous foundation principle of Lutheran theology: the spiritual priesthood of all believers.

These principles are basic for all Lutheran education. They constitute a spiritual dynamic which, when properly understood and applied, can and will transform the whole educational program.

Applications to and Implications for Education

Education here refers not merely to the subject of "Education" as a department in a college; it refers to the whole field of educational instruction at all levels and in various types of programs. No better introduction could be made to the educational implications of the above-noted Christian principles than to quote part of the *Report of the Oxford World Conference on Life and Work* in 1930: "The Church's largest contribution to education, like her supreme ministry to human life, is her Gospel with its interpretation of existence and its inspiration to live worthily. Where life is without meaning, education becomes futile. Where it (life) is ignobly conceived, education is debased. Where it (life) is viewed in the light of God's purpose in Christ, it assumes divine significance. . . . It is all important that the Gospel should supply the presuppositions of all education, by whatever agency it is given, and create the spiritual atmosphere which pervades every institution of learning."

Related to the Aim (Goals) of Education

1. The ultimate purpose of Lutheran education is the glorifying of God. "Whether you eat or drink, or whatever you do, do all to the glory of God" (I Cor. 10:31).

2. The student should be developed in all his powers of reason, emotion, and will for the glory of God, for his own welfare, and

in the interest of his fellow men. Without the continual and integrated development of the student in this manner, he becomes a warped personality.

3. Christian education will aim at developing an appreciative and intelligent stewardship of all knowledge and all skills. While some knowledge is appreciated for its own sake, generally knowledge and skill are means to larger ends.

4. Since a God of love created man to be in fellowship with him and in companionship with his fellow men, education will aim to develop man as an understanding, sympathetic, helpful, loving social personality.

5. Christian education has the responsibility of bringing the student to a realization of his fallen (sinful) status and to an acceptance of the divine grace whereby he may be restored to the divine image, from which he fell, and whereby in him may be fulfilled God's redeeming purpose.

6. Christian education, being grounded in the life-transforming power of the gospel, has as a central purpose the development of Christian character, achieved through the operation in life and the expression through life of a set of attitudes determined by and integrated about an ideal character, even the character and life of Jesus Christ. Recognizing the character of Jesus as beyond full attainment in this life by human beings, daily subject to sin and in need of forgiveness, nevertheless the Christian educator would have his students grow more and more into the likeness of Jesus Christ, until in another clime they may attain unto the fulness of "the perfecting of the saints."

Related to the Levels, Types, and Control of Education

1. The child as a creation of God belongs to God but is given to parents who have a God-given responsibility to train him up in the way he should go. Parents and teachers, appointed or

approved by the parents, are God's representatives for the development of children. Of course, any power assumed by parent and teacher must be limited by the will and spirit of God. So Paul urged, "Fathers, do not provoke your children to anger, but bring them up in the discipline and instruction of the Lord" (Eph. 6:4).

2. What Christian parents cannot do alone they have the right and duty to ask the church, the fellowship of believers, to do for them. So the church will organize, maintain, and support schools of various types in accordance with need and opportunity. This assumes that these schools will be quality schools, and that the presence of the Christian motive and spirit will be so definite and clear as to more than justify the church's expenditures (as well as the parents' expenditures) for such schools.

3. The state, after the parents and the church, is an order authorized by God to promote the temporal welfare of the people. The state is distinguished from the church, but since both are ordained by God there is not absolute separation. The state has been likened to the Law, and the church to the Gospel—both necessary, both different, but both not absolutely separate. Thus, the state has also a responsibility in the field of education, as a means for the moral development of its citizens. In a nation in which all citizens are Christians, the state would see to it that religion would be a definite part of the curriculum and life of the school. In a multireligious state, such as the United States, the problem of Christian instruction is a perennial issue.

Since both church and state are ordained of God, there should be complete co-operation in matters pertaining to the temporal and moral welfare of the people. The United States has the problem of deciding to what extent the federal government and the respective states should be engaged in the work of formal education.

4. Since the press, radio, television, and movies can be powers

for good or evil in the lives of Christian people, the church has the responsibility of making its evaluations known and of extending such influence through Christian leaders as will make these agencies instruments for good.

5. Since much of effective and inspiring teaching resides in the moral and spiritual qualities of the teacher, the church has responsibility for the preparation of personnel to serve the schools of the church and of the state. Even though most lasting influences are exerted by teachers in the elementary and secondary schools of church and state, it is not sufficient to stop there. The church should review from time to time its responsibility in developing programs for the graduate training of men and women to be qualified to teach in colleges, universities, theological seminaries, and other professional schools.

Related to Methods in Lutheran Education

1. The method will always be related to the general purpose of education and of an educational program, to the special aim of a particular course or subject, and to the status and life goal of the student (Eph. 4:11-16).

2. Lutheran education will be *directive* in a definite manner and to a definite degree. "Train up a child in the way he should go, and when he is old he will not depart from it" (Prov. 22:6). The Christian does not develop when a child is allowed to express merely his native attitudes and wishes; that has been and always will be the way of the jungle. The Scriptures and our experience repeatedly confirm the necessity for direction in achieving moral and spiritual development. In fact, growth in the grace of God requires response to the guiding Holy Spirit.

3. Lutheran education will be *transmissive* and *creative*. There is a body of facts and ideas which the student should learn. Just as the budding scientist is indoctrinated with facts and ideas be-

fore he can progress in his research, so the growing Christian must accept certain facts and ideas for his own development. Indoctrination by the church is no worse than indoctrination by science.

But the Lutheran church contends that education must be more than the mere intellectual grasp of facts and principles (more than a *Kopf und Maulglaube*—a head-and-mouth faith); Christian education must be creative and dynamic, even going beyond what may be comprehended at the moment by reason. Observation of Christians and experience with them give much desirable information for the direction of the Christian life, but much more is given through a correct interpretation of and meditation upon the Scriptures, the prayer life, and the work of the Holy Spirit. *Lutherans do not submit the mysteries of faith to the rules of reason.* There are some things to be believed which at the time are not comprehended by reason. This is where Lutherans differ radically from those who say that "nothing is to be believed that cannot be grasped and understood by reason."

4. The teacher in Lutheran education will teach *liberally*. Teaching liberally means teaching with a mind open to new truth in one's own field and to truth in all other fields. Teaching liberally means teaching with the consciousness that God is the God of truth and that he may reveal some new truth at any time.

5. The teacher in Lutheran education will teach *Christianly*. This word is used by Narum who says: "It is not enough that a course is given in a Christian college, or that the instructor is a professing Christian. It is necessary for the instructor to become aware of the implications of Christianity for his study, and to teach this relationship."[7]

Too frequently, Christian teachers in colleges use the outlines and subject-matter of courses studied in the graduate schools of

[7] Ditmanson, Hong, and Quanbeck, eds., *Christian Faith and the Liberal Arts* (Minneapolis: Augsburg Publishing House, 1960), p. 114.

universities without any conception of the application to or implication of the Christian faith for the course.

Related to Subject Fields in Higher Education

It is not desirable or convenient for this lecturer to set up a proposed ideal curriculum for the Lutheran college, but it is desirable and necessary to attempt to indicate the applications of the Christian faith for and in certain subject fields. Time and space do not permit an elaboration, but the readers who may be college teachers in these subject areas will be able to make their own elaborations.

Ontology

1. God is the Creator and Sustainer and Saviour of the universe and all therein. He is the first and ultimate Cause.

2. The relationship of God and the universe, spirit and matter, soul and body, is not one of absolute separation, as the deists would say. Nor is it one of elimination of one by the other, as both the pantheists and materialists would say. Rather, this relationship is a unity in duality, as the theist claims. The Creator manifests himself through the creation; the spirit works with and through the material; the soul (mind) operates through a body.

This concept explains the miracles of the Bible and allows for miracles at any time. God, the Creator of all things, is Lord of nature, according to whose power he may reveal his purpose in some unique natural event. This interpretation has very definite significance for the Lutheran interpretation of the Sacraments—the Word and the water, the Word and the elements.

3. The creation is "very good," and the concepts of sacred and secular are not applicable thereto. Wherein the creation has been marred by sin, it awaits redemption (Rom. 8:22, 23).

Epistemology

1. Since God is the God of truth, God and the universe are knowable and man is knowledgeable. Being created in the image of God, man can know God to some degree.

2. God has revealed and does reveal himself in his creation, in his Incarnation in Jesus Christ, and through the operation of the Holy Spirit.

3. God reveals truth to man as he wills and as man is able to receive it. Truth is not obtained by the rationalist or intellectualist through the operation of reason; rather, truth is attained when the whole man is confronted by God in Christ.

4. Truth is given to man in order that he may *do* it. This Biblical concept is quite different from that of ancient, medieval, and modern philosophers. It is quite common for the psalmist to speak of walking in the truth (Ps. 26:3; 86:11). Hezekiah says, "I have walked before thee in truth" (Isa. 38:3, K.J.V.). So also in the New Testament truth is generally associated with action. Jesus said, "I am the way, and the truth, and the life" (John 14:6). John wrote, "He who does what is true comes to the light, that it may be clearly seen that his deeds have been wrought in God" (John 3:21). Also, Paul speaks of the penalty for not obeying the truth (Rom. 2:8) and, likewise, Peter writes, "Having purified your souls by your obedience to the truth for a sincere love of the brethren, love one another earnestly from the heart" (I Pet. 1:22).

Language

Language is the medium through which God communicated his gospel of love to man and through which man may continue this communication. Such communication requires accuracy and definiteness in the use of language and of the knowledge of literature, especially the Scriptures. It more than justifies all the labors of Biblical language students, and all the varied translations.

History

In the field of history we see the operation of God's work of salvation and the coming of his Kingdom. An understanding of the past gives a clearer understanding of the future.

Music

Through music God may be adored, his name praised, and his creation and redemption honored.

Physical Sciences

1. Man's studies of all aspects of the natural world are ways whereby man may read God's thoughts after him and understand more fully the intricacies and mysteries of the physical world.

2. The Word of God gives meaning to all the sciences, for through them the Word may be further understood.

Social Sciences, Including Psychology

1. The true nature or measure of man is not understood apart from the truth of man's creation in the image of God, the reality of the Fall, and redemption through God's grace. This viewpoint gives a depth dimension in anthropology, psychology, and sociology, and removes the superficial optimism of much philosophy through the centuries and of most modern theology.

2. Redemption by God's grace gives man a heightened sense of personal responsibility. Lutheran education does not forget the individual in an age of mass production and mechanical uniformity. God deals with the individual through personal faith rather than that of the group or the mass.

3. Man's redemption places him in right relation with both God and his fellow men. This fact has significance for the democratic way of life. Such elements of democracy as freedom, equality, fraternity have new meaning through Christian faith.

4. The doctrine of the universal priesthood of believers directs

attention to the importance of man's being prepared for his particular calling or lifework.

5. All men, without reference to race, nation, sex, or economic status, but merely because of the fact that in Christ God's grace is open for them, have the special privileges of children of God.

Axiology (Theory of Values)

1. Man, viewed in light of his relationship to God in Christ and to his fellow men, becomes the measure of all things.

2. Though man needs the state for his social and political welfare, the state was made for man and not man for the state; though education helps man to develop his capacities, education was made for man and not man for education; and, though man needs vocation to actualize his God-given talents, vocation was made for man and not man for vocation.

Theology

1. Theology, man's systematized understanding of God and of his relation to man and of God's revelation of himself to man, is both a basic and a climactic subject to be studied in some form by all students.

2. The Holy Scriptures constitute the chief textbook for this study, with supplementary material found in the Book of Nature and the Book of Humanity.

CONCLUSION

It is evident that Lutheran theology can make a difference in all aspects of education. The Lutheran church needs to encourage Lutheran educators, wherever they may serve, to become more fully informed about the theology of Lutheran education, to the end that their labors may be to the glory of God and for the development of their students in that truth which makes them free.

II

VENTURING IN
THEOLOGICAL EDUCATION

Although theological seminaries come last in the sequence of the church's possible educational program—elementary, secondary, collegiate, and theological—theological education was really first in the mind of the church and of individuals interested in higher education. Of course, elementary education in the early colonies was necessary as a beginning. Seldom is it explicitly pointed out that the primary motive in the founding of Harvard College in 1636 was theological and ecclesiastical. It is true the founders wanted to "advance learning and perpetuate it to Posterity," but—and here's the motive—they dreaded "to leave an illiterate ministry to the Churches when our present ministers shall lie in the Dust." President Josiah Quincy was honest enough to admit that Harvard had fulfilled the design of its founders in that, during the period 1636 to 1692, it had been "conducted as a theological institution."[1] Tewksbury, in his valuable volume *The Founding of American Colleges and Universities Before the Civil War,* indicates that the same theological motive was dominant in the founding of fourteen other schools in various sections of the country.[2]

[1] Josiah Quincy, *The History of Harvard University,* 1840. Vol. I, p. 3. And yet Morrison does not wish to think of the early Harvard as a "theological seminary." Cf. S. E. Morrison, *The Founding of Harvard College* (Cambridge: Harvard University Press, 1935), pp. 8, 247-248, 250.

[2] Donald G. Tewksbury, *The Founding of American Colleges and Universities Before the Civil War* (New York: Columbia University Press, 1932), pp. 81-84.

How did the Lutherans venture in theological education? How did they try to furnish ministers for their churches? Frankly, it was not by establishing educational institutions with a theological motive and then allowing those schools to become more or less secular. The positive answer involves the efforts of individual pastors and the founding of theological seminaries.

INDIVIDUAL EFFORTS

Dutch Lutherans along the Hudson River in 1623 and 1625 and Swedish Lutherans along the Delaware River in 1638 apparently gave no or little thought to the matter of training men for their pulpits.[3] When the Germans migrated to the United States during the eighteenth century, definite steps were taken by such men as Henry Melchior Muhlenberg to provide a school and a teacher for each congregation or groups of congregations, with instruction in the Bible and the Catechism and general education. All of this pointed toward a trained native ministry. In 1765 Muhlenberg received a sum of money toward the establishment of a "high school" or seminary. Various plans for an institution did not work out and Muhlenberg was compelled to give private tutoring to individuals interested in serving as pastors, since by 1771 he reported seventy congregations in Pennsylvania and nearby, and thirty Lutheran congregations elsewhere.

Another one who worked hard and planned carefully for the establishment of a Lutheran seminary prior to the Revolution was John Christopher Kunze, who had studied at Halle and Leipsic. He organized "The Society for the Propagation of Christianity and Useful Knowledge among the Germans in America" as a means of supporting a theological school. A school was started in Philadelphia in February, 1773. But with the Germans opposing

[3] A. R. Wentz, *History of Gettysburg Theological Seminary* (Philadelphia: United Lutheran Publication House, 1926), p. 18. See also pp. 18-63 for detailed information about early efforts to provide an American-trained ministry.

England in various matters, it is not surprising to learn that the British troops occupying Philadelphia in 1777 took over "the very building in which the Seminary was held." Later Kunze was called to New York, where his scholarship was recognized and he was elected both a regent of Columbia University and a member of the faculty. This, he hoped, might be a means whereby he could start a seminary for Lutheran pastors, but it was in vain.

The need for American-trained Lutheran pastors grew year by year. Lutheran congregations were organized in many states with the continued growth of Lutheran immigration. Before congregations were strong enough to establish an educational institution which was worthy of the name, Lutheran pastors could not rest with the prospect of an untrained ministry. The only possibility open was for those pastors with special talent to begin tutoring candidates for the ministry, whom they sought out and taught.

Most of these tutor-pastors, we read, were no ordinary men. Some had received the Doctor of Divinity degree from the University of Pennsylvania and Columbia University at a time when this degree was an unusual honor. Their work was thorough; their examinations severe; their standards were high. Many housed the candidates in their own homes. In spite of their heavy burdens as pastors, they gave extra hours for the sake of an American-trained ministry. No doubt all of them looked to the day when theological seminaries would be established in various sections of the country.

THE FOUNDING OF LUTHERAN SEMINARIES[4]

It is greatly regretted that the limits of time for the delivery of these lectures and even of space for their printing prevent giving historical sketches of all Lutheran seminaries established

[4] The material for these sketches was taken from official catalogues and histories, supplemented by correspondence with the seminaries.

through the generations. Such sketches would have been monotonous to some, informing to others, and most interesting to those who with imagination could see the expansion of Lutheran church bodies and their venturing in theological education, north and south, east and west, through the United States and Canada. Here we must be satisfied with glimpses at certain situations and an exhibit of existing Lutheran seminaries with their names and present locations, dates of founding, and the supporting church bodies. Several closed seminaries are not even mentioned.

The first Lutheran theological seminary to be established in America was *Hartwick Seminary* in 1797 in the village of Hartwick Seminary, near Cooperstown, New York. The will of John Christopher Hartwick, who came to America in 1745 and died in 1796, provided for the establishment of a ministerial evangelical school for the spreading of evangelical Christianity among the heathen. The first professor was John Christopher Kunze, mentioned previously as a man of recognized ability, much interested in theological education in Philadelphia and New York City. The school produced some prominent Lutheran leaders, even though the enrollment was never large. In 1930 it was moved to Brooklyn, then to New York City, and finally discontinued in 1946, with its assets used to establish a Hartwick Seminary Foundation at Hartwick College and the academic records going to the Philadelphia Seminary. There is a sense in which Hartwick Seminary might be considered the first Protestant theological seminary established in America, since it antedates Andover Seminary (1808), the Dutch Reformed Seminary at New Brunswick (1810), and the Presbyterian Seminary at Princeton (1812); but it was the fourth to obtain a building in 1815.

Since the need for a theological seminary was increasing year by year, and since individuals and groups had failed to establish a seminary in Pennsylvania and New York, it is not surprising that the General Synod, organized in 1820, took prompt action looking toward the establishment of a seminary. This was done in September, 1826, at Gettysburg, Pennsylvania, with the Rev. S. S. Schmucker as the professor in charge. The members of the first board of directors were chosen by the General Synod as representatives of the various district synods, but thereafter all directors were and have been elected by the district synods supporting the seminary. Since the *Lutheran Theological Seminary at Gettysburg, Pennsylvania,* as it was named, was the first permanent seminary to be established in America, this method of establishing the school is interesting.

Lutheranism was growing and district synods were being organized, but Lutherans had learned that to establish a seminary required the united approval and support of many congregations. The Rev. John Bachman of Charleston, South Carolina, persistently urged the establishment of a seminary in the South. Finally, in 1830 the Synod of South Carolina took action authorizing the establishment of a theological seminary and a classical academy. In that year the institution was opened at Pomaria, South Carolina. Unfortunate conditions, including the Civil War and inadequate financial support, caused the school to be moved more than any other Lutheran seminary in America. From Pomaria it moved to Lexington, South Carolina, in 1855; thence to Newberry in 1856; thence to Walhalla in 1868; thence to Mt. Pleasant, North Carolina, in 1898, with John Alfred Morehead as dean; and finally to Columbia, South Carolina, in 1911—its present desirable location. The school's official name is *Lutheran Theological Southern Seminary.*

In 1830 Lutherans west of the Allegheny Mountains, the Joint Synod of Ohio, established a school to train pastors at Canton, but the next year moved it to Columbus where it has remained and is known as *Capital Seminary,* because of its relation with Capital University. Its official name is *Evangelical Lutheran Theological Seminary.*

By this time immigrants from Germany had come to the United States and settled in states farther west. So it was in 1839 that *Concordia Seminary*, as a classical school and school of theology, was founded at Altenburg, Perry County, Missouri, by the Rev. Ottomar Fuerbringer. In 1849 it was moved to St. Louis and in 1926 relocated just outside Clayton, Missouri.

It is not surprising that the English Evangelical Lutheran Synod of Ohio was stimulated into action and in 1842 voted to establish a literary and theological institution. In May, 1844, a young pastor, the Rev. Ezra Keller, started the instruction of four candidates for the ministry at Wooster, Ohio, and continued with them when the school was established at Springfield in 1845, which is the date assigned to the founding of both Wittenberg College and its theological department, so-called at that time. Later the department was known as Wittenberg Theological Seminary, and after 1907 it received the name of *Hamma Divinity School* of Wittenberg College in tribute to Dr. and Mrs. Michael Wolfe Hamma. Today the school is an integral part of Wittenberg University.

During the period 1840 to 1870 German groups in east-central states, Indiana, Illinois, Iowa, Minnesota, and Wisconsin, were rather active in venturing in theological education. Without being able to give certain desirable details, we can only say that *Concordia Theological Seminary* was established at Fort Wayne, Indiana, in 1846 as a practical seminary; moved to St. Louis in 1861, "in order to make the so-called practical seminary all the more efficient" by affiliation with the other Concordia; and then moved to Springfield, Illinois, during 1874-1875. *Wartburg Theological Seminary* was founded in 1854 by The Synod of Iowa at Dubuque, Iowa; moved to St. Sebald in 1858; thence to Galena, Illinois; then to Mendota, Illinois, where it functioned from 1874 to 1889; and then returned to Dubuque. The Joint Synod of Ohio established a *Luther Seminary* in 1884 at Afton, Minnesota; moved it to St. Paul in 1893; and then merged it with Wartburg at Dubuque, when the Synods of Ohio, Buffalo, and Iowa merged in 1930. The Wisconsin Synod opened an institution with a department of theology in 1865 at Watertown; moved the students to St. Louis Concordia Seminary in 1870; re-opened their school in 1878 at Milwaukee; thence moved it in 1893 to Wauwatosa; and finally in 1929 to Thiensville, where the *Wisconsin Lutheran Seminary* is now located.

Around the middle of the nineteenth century Swedish immigrants came to Illinois, Iowa, and Minnesota. Those coming to Illinois had the spiritual supervision of Pastor Lars P. Esbjörn. The pastors who came with these Swedish immigrants were graduates of the university and anxious for an educated ministry. They associated themselves with the Synod of Northern Illinois in support of an educational institution at Springfield known as Illinois State University, of which faculty Pastor Esbjörn was a member. Because of various factors, especially differences in theological points of view, a new synod and a new school were formed in 1860, both receiving the name *Augustana*. The school was located in Chicago, with Pastor Esbjörn as president until 1863, when it was moved to Paxton. Then in 1875 it was relocated at Rock Island, where it has remained. Until 1948 the seminary functioned under the same corporation and constitution as the college, but in that year the seminary obtained its own charter, constitution, board of directors, funds, and administration.

While the Lutherans in the east-central states were much concerned about theological education, those in Pennsylvania and Maryland were torn with tensions—theological, American-German, and personal. The Rev. Benjamin Kurtz, a pastor of the Maryland Synod who had worked hard for the Gettysburg Seminary, wanted a school where men "thoroughly converted and devoutly pious, of good natural sense and robust health, not emaciated by sedentary habits" could take a shorter or longer course of study and thus hasten the filling of the need for more men for the ministry. Since Gettysburg would not yield to certain demands of Kurtz, he went to Selinsgrove, Pennsylvania, and in 1858 established a "missionary institute," with himself as superintendent. As a department of theology of Susquehanna University, it was continued until 1933, when it suspended operations rather than merge with either Gettysburg or Philadelphia Seminary.

The oldest Lutheran synod in America, the Ministerium of Pennsylvania, was not satisfied with the seminary at Gettysburg and finally established its own in 1864 at Philadelphia by electing the Rev. C. F. Schaeffer, its own professor at Gettysburg Seminary, as the first regular professor, who took with him all, or most, of the German students. Thus was founded the *Lutheran Theological Seminary* at Philadelphia.

The first seminary founded by Norwegians was at Marshall, Wisconsin, in 1869 as *Augsburg Seminary*. The Norwegian Synod established *Luther Seminary* at Madison, Wisconsin, in 1876. After mergers of various church bodies and their seminaries, which is a complicated story, today we find Augsburg Seminary in Minneapolis, supported by the Lutheran Free Church, and *Luther Theological Seminary* in St. Paul, supported formerly by the Evangelical Lutheran Church, now by the American Lutheran Church.

Danish Lutheran groups were active in theological education in the 1880's and 1890's. The Danish Evangelical Lutheran Church Association, commonly known as the "Blair Synod," was organized in 1884 and started *Trinity Seminary* at Blair, Nebraska, in conjunction with Dana College. In 1956 this school was moved to the campus of *Wartburg Seminary* and merged therewith when the American Lutheran Church was formed in 1960.

Other Danish groups were thinking of theological education in Wisconsin and Iowa, but finally in 1896 established *Grand View*

College and Seminary as one institution at Des Moines, Iowa. In 1952 the seminary was separated from the college administratively and functionally. The American Evangelical Lutheran Church, renamed from the Danish Lutheran Church, voted in 1959 to affiliate this seminary with the Chicago Lutheran Theological Seminary at Maywood, Illinois. This was done in September, 1960, as the church looked forward to a larger merger in 1962.

During this period of American expansion the General Council decided to establish a seminary in Chicago and invited the Augustana Synod to move its seminary from Rock Island. This offer was refused, since it was considered "an occasion for division and separation." The *Chicago Lutheran Theological Seminary* was established in 1891 in Chicago and moved to Maywood in 1920.

While the General Council expanded its theological education to Chicago, the General Synod expanded to Atchison, Kansas, and established *Western Theological Seminary* in October, 1895. In 1910 the General Synod transferred its ownership and control of the seminary to Midland College, located in the same city. Both were moved to Fremont, Nebraska, in 1919, with the seminary as a department of the college. Finally, in 1949 the seminary was separated from the college under the name of *Central Lutheran Theological Seminary,* with its own constitution and board of directors.

The Finnish Evangelical Church in America ventured in theological education in 1904 by establishing *Suomi College and Seminary* at Hancock, Michigan.

The Synod of the Northwest established a seminary in 1920 at Fargo, North Dakota, but, recognizing that this location was not desirable, moved it to Minneapolis in 1921 with the name *Northwestern Lutheran Theological Seminary.*

In Canada two synods, the Canada Synod and the Synod of

Central Canada, opened *Waterloo Seminary* in 1911. It is now one of the schools of Waterloo Lutheran University, at Waterloo, Ontario. In the western province of Alberta, *Lutheran College and Seminary* was established at Edmonton in 1913 and moved to Saskatoon in 1915, with definite theological instruction starting in 1918. In 1933 the academy and college departments were discontinued and funds and facilities were used to develop the seminary. In 1939 the Evangelical Lutheran Church was granted permission to begin theological instruction on the same campus; professors and students shared all the advantages and facilities of the *Lutheran Seminary*. In 1945 the Augustana Lutheran Church and in 1949 the American Lutheran Church agreed also to co-operate with the United Lutheran Church in theological education at Saskatoon, each supplying a professor and students and assisting in the total support of the school. *Here for the first time in American Lutheranism, four different Lutheran bodies co-operated in theological education at one institution.* However, in 1946, the Evangelical Lutheran Church moved its seminary, *Luther Theological Seminary,* to a location a few blocks from the University of Saskatchewan and only a mile from the *Lutheran Seminary,* with which some co-operation was continued. When church mergers became realistic, these four church bodies recognized that it was neither reasonable nor economic to have two small Lutheran seminaries in Saskatoon. So in September, 1958, the two seminaries began functioning as one, on the property of the Lutheran Seminary (ULCA), from which the Luther Theological Seminary had withdrawn twelve years before. Each school maintains its own legal identity, with a common Lutheran faculty of theology and with each group's having its own responsible director.

The need for a Lutheran seminary on the west coast could not be denied, in spite of the closing of the Pacific Lutheran Seminary in Seattle in 1933. So Pacific Synod and the Pacific Southwest

Synod agreed to establish *The Pacific Lutheran Theological Seminary* at Berkeley, California, which was incorporated in 1950 and opened for instruction in 1952, with the Rev. Charles B. Foelsch as president.

In 1946 the Evangelical Lutheran Synod (formerly called The Norwegian Synod) resolved to open a full *theological department in Bethany College,* a junior college, at Mankato, Minnesota. The "Church of the Lutheran Confession" was organized in 1959. It established *Immanuel Lutheran College* with a theological department during the same year.

Because of its historical significance, it is proper to conclude this survey with a note on the founding of *The Lutheran School of Theology at Chicago* in the fall of 1962 when the articles of incorporation will be filed. This is the latest venture in Lutheran theological education and will mark the merger of Augustana Theological Seminary, Grand View Seminary, Suomi Seminary, and Chicago Lutheran Theological Seminary. Until a new location can be obtained and proper facilities developed, the school will be operated at two locations to be known as *The Lutheran School of Theology—Maywood Campus* and *The Lutheran School of Theology—Rock Island Campus.* Thus will be realized a plan of the General Council in 1893 for the establishment of a seminary at some *central* point "where the future ministry of our *English, German* and *Scandinavian* churches may be educated *together* in the unity of the common faith confessed and maintained by this body"[5] (italics supplied).

PRESENT STATUS OF LUTHERAN SEMINARIES

The brief historical sketches make up an interesting story of commitment, conflict, competition, and expansion in Lutheran theological education across the vast territories of Canada and

[5] General Council Minutes, 1893, p. 53.

the United States. It is now desirable to get a closer look at Lutheran theological education, but from a comprehensive point of view rather than the details of each school.

Interesting Figures

Lutheran theological education should be viewed within the framework of general theological education, which is no small business in America. In the *Handbook of Christian Higher Education (1940)*, Wickey and Anderson report that in 1938 there were 181 theological seminaries and departments and 26 training colleges and schools, making a total of 207 Protestant and independent theological training centers. The same year there were 101 major and 81 minor Roman Catholic seminaries. (Technically, the Catholic minor or preparatory seminaries should not be included as seminaries, since they are the equivalent of Protestant high schools and junior colleges preparing men for the ministry.) In 1960 the American Association of Theological Schools reported 122 accredited and associate members of Protestant and independent relationship, all requiring a four-year college education for candidacy for the B.D. degree. It is estimated that there are probably 50 additional theological or Bible schools and departments, used by certain denominations as training centers for their ministry. This means that from 1938 to 1960 there was a drop of some 35 theological and Bible schools among the Protestants. In 1960 the Roman Catholics reported 134 major seminaries—an increase of 33. They also reported 92 major-minor (a category not used in 1938) seminaries and 161 minor seminaries. These figures are sufficient to show that, even though church membership is increasing, Protestant theological schools have decreased at least 10% during a 22-year period, while the Catholics have increased their major seminaries 33%, and their major-minor and minor seminaries practically 200%.

As we turn to Lutheran seminaries, we note that *The Lutheran Church Year Book for 1919* listed 23 seminaries. The number had increased by only one in 1959, but during the intervening forty years there were several changes by closings, mergers, and new schools. However, at the end of 1962 the number is 20; the decrease of four is due to the merger of church bodies and the consequent realignment of seminaries. There is no question but that the 20 seminaries in 1962 are much stronger in faculty size and training, larger in enrollments, and better prepared with facilities for effective instruction than the 23 seminaries in 1919. The property value of these seminaries is $25,702,000, the endowments amount to $7,292,629, and the number of volumes in the libraries total 549,443. In the fall of 1961 the faculty members numbered 260 and the regular students for the ministry, 3,180. With the 492 postgraduate students and the 576 summer-school students, the total registration at the seminaries numbered 4,248.

Purpose and Policies

The purpose of all Lutheran seminaries may be summarized in the words of the constitution of the oldest existing Lutheran seminary, namely, Gettysburg: "To train men for the Christian ministry, especially for the Lutheran Church, and also to prepare competent men and women as leaders in Christian education and in other spheres of Christian service." Some constitutions state the purpose in fewer words; others, in more words.

However, there is a trend in theological education to state the aims on a somewhat broader base, not in constitutions but in catalogues. This is seen in the statement of Hamma Divinity School, which asserts its aims as:

1. To train men for service in the church as faithful, dedicated and competent ordained ministers of the Word of God.

2. To be a community for theological investigation and scholarship so as to be a center of intellectual life for the church.
3. To provide training for lay leaders and for those desiring to enter special service, such as directors of religious education, church musicians, parish business managers, and editors.
4. To prepare and stimulate students for further graduate study and research in all the disciplines of theology and the life of the church.
5. To engage in continuing conversation with other intellectual disciplines.
6. To conduct these activities so that students, having decided to dedicate their whole lives to the ministry, may grow in their love for God and neighbor.
7. To contribute by these functions to the total global mission and work of the church.

This statement is significant in that: (*a*) it recognizes that the seminary is the center of the intellectual life of the church; (*b*) it admits the necessity for further investigation and scholarship beyond the achievements of the past; (*c*) it declares that theology cannot be a discipline isolated from other intellectual disciplines; and (*d*) it relates the seminary to the whole global mission and program of the church.

Although there are a few non-Lutheran seminaries at present independent of any one church body, all of them have had direct or indirect relations with some church body in their early history and were governed by some definite policies of church relationship. Probably 95% of all non-Catholic theological seminaries are definitely related to some church body. In these cases generally a board of directors is selected or elected by the regional districts or synods of the church body. In some cases the church body selects the members of the board, or a church board of education may constitute the board of the seminary. The latest development in the relations of a national board of theological education to its church body and to its seminaries is seen in the regulations of the Board of Theological Education of the Lutheran Church in America, which legally comes into existence in 1962. Those regulations are interesting, since they spell out to a considerable degree the relations of such a national board to the national church body, the constituent synods, and the seminaries. The Board of Theological Education:

(1) manifests the church's concern for its theological seminaries, and, in general, the education of the ministry;

(2) recognizes the principle that each regional synod is responsible in whole or in part for a single seminary, and reports to the national church the ways in which each synod is fulfilling this responsibility;

(3) nominates from 20% to 40% of the total number of trustees of each seminary to be elected by the supporting synod or synods;

(4) makes recommendations or a master plan for location and areas of specialization of seminaries, including their establishment and relocation and the relationships of synods to the seminaries;

(5) establishes educational standards;

(6) gives supplementary financial support;

(7) administers scholarship and fellowship funds for theological education;

(8) counsels seminaries in the selection of teaching personnel;

(9) encourages and makes provision for postgraduate studies and other specialized studies in theology, either at existing institutions or otherwise as may be determined by the church;

(10) provides testing and counselling services for theological and pretheological students; and

(11) encourages and provides facilities for continued theological studies by pastors in service.

Such definite and clear-cut specifications help all concerned to know the varied responsibilities, and to plan and to co-operate accordingly without wondering whether such a step is or is not within the scope of duties and co-operation and without running to some superior body for permission to do that which always should have been self-evident.

Standards

Any seminary may adopt any standards of admission and graduation which it may wish, of course with the approval of the supporting church body, if such there be. But if a seminary wishes to be an accredited school, it must follow the standards of the American Association of Theological Schools, the only accrediting association for theological seminaries in America. According to these standards, admission requires graduation from a four-year college, or the equivalent thereof, based upon four years of work beyond secondary education. Students from a nonaccredited college are admitted on academic probation or the passing of a general examination on the applicant's pretheological studies. The course of study in a seminary is normally three years of two semesters each, or their equivalent, beyond the college bachelor's degree. The curriculum of an accredited seminary presupposes a broad and sound basis in the liberal arts and sciences, and includes thorough instruction in four areas: biblical, historical, theological, and practical (functional). The faculty should include at least six professors, competent as scholars and teachers, having a weekly teaching load of not more than twelve hours per instructor. It is assumed that there are not fewer than twenty-five students. The facilities in land, buildings, library, and finances must be adequate to carry out the program of the school. The Association accredits schools "upon academic criteria without reference to doctrinal position or ecclesiastical affiliation."

Of the twenty-three Lutheran seminaries existing at the beginning of 1962, ten were fully accredited and three more were associate members of the American Association of Theological Schools. The accredited seminaries were: Gettysburg, Philadelphia, Southern, Hamma, Capital, Chicago, Augustana, Wartburg, Luther, and Northwestern.

The associate members were: Concordia (St. Louis), Central,

and Pacific (Berkeley). Playing the prophet, the author feels that it is likely that two of these associates will be accredited members by 1964.

Facilities

The facilities of the Lutheran accredited seminaries have become quite satisfactory, though not elaborate or luxurious. The unaccredited schools are generally weak in some of the following: finances, especially for faculty salaries; number of properly trained faculty members; adequate number of usable volumes in the library; certain physical facilities; and perhaps some other standards as well.

Programs

The curricula of Lutheran seminaries are not identical, not even those of the seminaries belonging to the same church body. In response to a request for uniform curricula in all ten seminaries of the ULCA, the Board of Higher Education of that church replied that seminaries as "professional schools need the right and opportunity to experiment in various courses looking toward making their training programs more effective. Uniformity would prevent this." However, in 1948 that same board did prepare, with the co-operation of the seminaries, a standard core curriculum including the purpose of theological education, statements of objectives and methods according to the different fields of the curriculum, and a suggested distribution of credits within and among the fields of study. Especially significant were the statements of the objectives and methods to be followed in the various fields of the curriculum. These in themselves give a unity and a uniformity to theological education without deterring professors from manifesting their ability and ingenuity in developing new courses. Something of this sort would be of special significance if it were worked out for all Lutheran seminaries.[6]

The intern or vicar year is winning approval in Lutheran seminaries and their supporting church bodies. The plan calls for a student's going at the end of the second year to a parish with a pastor who will co-operate in helping to orientate the student to the whole parish program. A director or supervisor or counsellor from the seminary visits the parish once or twice a year to confer with both pastor and student, who also send reports to the seminary monthly or quarterly. Students who object to this program admit, after experiencing it, that it is most valuable and see its importance as a required part of seminary training.

The Augustana Lutheran Church since 1934 and The Lutheran Church-Missouri Synod since 1946 have required this program of their seminary students on an organized plan. However, Concordia Seminary (St. Louis) did send out students in 1932 to do various types of church work. The former American Lutheran Church and the Evangelical Lutheran Church started a program somewhat later on an optional basis. The ULCA approved a plan in 1954, but the constituent synods were slow in accepting it, except the Pacific (Northwest) and the Pacific Southwest Synods, who made it mandatory for ordination. This, in turn, made it mandatory for graduation at the Pacific Lutheran Theological Seminary, at least for students related to those two synods. It may become mandatory at 60% of the Lutheran seminaries before 1970. To make the program more effective, more definite standards for placement, supervision, and direction need to be approved.

The significance of this intern program for the Lutheran church is not that Lutheran church bodies were leaders in the intern or vicar program, but that, as Dr. Vernon L. Strempke, formerly associate secretary of the Board of Higher Education,

[6] See Minutes of the United Lutheran Church in America, 1948, pp. 460-465.

ULCA, now professor at Central Lutheran Theological Seminary, wrote in a personal letter, "the Lutheran church has succeeded in emphasizing the educational value of the internship more than any other church body. Practical experience often has been made available to students primarily for the monetary returns, but not by Lutheran seminaries."

The intern year should not be confused with the clinical year. The clinical year movement began about 1925-1930, and has been developed by the Council for Clinical Training and the Institute for Pastoral Care. Both Gettysburg and Philadelphia seminaries have held membership in the council, but no other Lutheran seminaries and only a few other Protestant seminaries have belonged or now belong. The relation of Lutherans to this movement is believed, according to Dr. Strempke, to have "developed a denominational or church consciousness among the training groups, with the consequence there has developed a close relationship with seminaries on the part of the training centers. This Lutheran involvement has also resulted in Lutheran training centers which are accredited either by the aforesaid groups or by the National Lutheran Council's Division of Welfare."

Dr. Carl Plack, of the National Lutheran Council's staff, played a prominent part in the development of accredited Lutheran agencies. Concordia Seminary at St. Louis has organized a good clinical training program with centers in St. Louis hospitals, which, it appears, is well integrated into the curriculum of the seminary. It is possible for other Lutheran seminaries to be related in a similar manner to training centers in their communities.

It is likely that the Chicago Lutheran Theological Seminary pioneered in the field of postgraduate work through its extramural program started in 1896, whereby pastors under direction from the seminary would read and report on a large number of volumes in various theological fields, with concentration in one, and after passing certain examinations would be granted the degrees of

Master of Sacred Theology or Doctor of Sacred Theology. This program was replaced by the present Division of Graduate Studies. At present both Chicago and Concordia, St. Louis, (since 1922) have students in residence working for doctorates. For many years the Philadelphia (1913) and Gettysburg (1928) seminaries have offered postgraduate courses to pastors who come to the campuses one or two days a week.

In recent years there has developed in some Lutheran seminaries the program for lay workers in the church. Gettysburg Seminary was no doubt the first to offer a special program for women to earn the master's degree in Christian education on the basis of two years of full-time study. Some of the courses are the same as those of the students preparing for the ministry, including the study of the Scriptures, Christian history, and the teachings of Christianity. Chicago (Maywood) Seminary adopted its program in 1948. The Pacific Lutheran Theological Seminary in its recently adopted program adds "workshop training in the functional activities of the church. . . . Weekends and the summertime are expected to be devoted to on-the-job training," usually in a normal congregational setting. Concordia Seminary (St. Louis) has inaugurated a Master of Arts in Religion program in its School for Graduate Studies. It requires that forty-eight quarter hours of advanced work be completed within eight years.

The master's degree in theology for ministers (S.T.M. or Th.M.) is offered by a large percentage of Lutheran seminaries. There appears to be a growing interest in advanced studies on the part of ministers, and the seminaries meeting the demand.

Special types of programs valuable to non-resident students have been developed. For many years Philadelphia Seminary sent a team of professors to certain centers on the territory of their supporting synods for the purpose of delivering a series of lectures. Special conferences and convocations are held by most of the seminaries rather regularly on an annual basis. The Gettysburg annual Seminary Week is outstanding in the number of pastors attending and in the types of lecturers obtained. Recently special institutes were started at ULCA seminaries. The Institutes on Preaching initiated by the Board of Higher Education, ULCA, in the summer of 1956 were so successful that pastors, the seminaries, and the board saw the value of "in-service study of theology" by pastors and the need for a larger program of summer institutes. It is likely that institutes of various types will increase greatly in numbers and be held in all sections of the church territory. Such programs can transform the attitudes, the study habits, the thinking, and effectiveness of all pastors.

This picture of the present status of Lutheran theological seminaries indicates dedication to the training of the parish ministry, alertness to new avenues for theological education, and desire for the maintenance of the best possible standards. Between the bright colors are some shadows (intimations) of inadequate support and low salaries and some better-trained professors. For Lutheran theological education there can be the highest motivation in asking for funds and in making grants. Lutheran church bodies cannot afford to aid their seminaries on a piecemeal basis; all seminary needs should be met fully and in light of long-range programs. This applies equally to current expenses and capital expenditures. Seminaries are the church in theological education. Inadequately supported seminaries are a manifestation of a weakness in the life of the church. If the Lutheran church is really interested in education, it will prove it in the manner in which theological seminaries are maintained and developed.

PRODUCT AND PROBLEMS

Can the Lutheran church be proud of her venture in theological education? Has there been a definite contribution to theological thought by the American Lutheran theologian? Have Lutheran theologians looked beyond the confines of their denomination and allowed their light to shine? Are there persistent problems calling for a united Lutheranism? These are a few of the questions which need consideration, even though they may not be answered in these pages.

A Well-Educated Ministry

Lutheran seminaries have stood for high standards in the education of the ministry. When the Conference of Theological Schools set itself up as an accrediting agency and changed its name to the American Association of Theological Schools in 1936, the Lutherans present urged that certain courses be set down as prerequisites for admission to seminaries, but they were opposed by representatives of some other denominations who did not want to require graduation from a four-year college as a prerequisite. In this instance the Lutherans stood with the leaders from the large nondenominational seminaries.

It is generally known that the Religious Census of 1926 showed that in the United Lutheran Church in America 81.9% and in the Augustana Lutheran Church 85.4% of the ministers were graduates of both college and seminary. This was the highest for any major denomination in America. Some other denominations showed these figures: The Reformed Church in the U.S., 81.2%; the Presbyterian Church in the U.S., 69.3%; the Protestant Episcopal Church, 61.4%; and the Methodist Episcopal Church, 24%. Since 1934, with the publication of the Brown and May study, *The Education of American Ministers,* many denominations have stiffened their requirements for the education of their ministry. But there are no facts available to show that any church body today has surpassed the percentage of the Lutheran church. Of all present Lutheran ministers, probably more than 85% are graduates of colleges (church and others), and 95% are graduates of Lutheran seminaries. In a release by Dr. George Harkins, Secretary of the ULCA, on January 26, 1962, it was reported that of ULCA pastors 72% are graduates of *church* colleges and 93% are graduates of *denominational* seminaries.

But the question has been raised as to whether the students at our seminaries might not obtain a better theological education if they were allowed to attend another seminary during their second year, and even during their third year. This was explicitly brought to the attention of the United Lutheran Church convention in 1954. The inquirer wanted to know whether a uniform curriculum in all ten seminaries of the ULCA "would tend to make it possible for a student to take advantage of more than one seminary faculty, without having to spend an additional year or two in a graduate school." The Board of Higher Education gave an extensive reply to this inquiry, after consulting the faculties of its ten seminaries, in its report to the 1956 convention of the ULCA, which was to the effect that "it is undesirable to establish such a [unified] curriculum" in all ten seminaries and went on to indicate some fifteen problems involved.

However, this did not deny the desirability of some students' taking a year at another school other than the one from which they desire to graduate. Students in Europe go from one theological faculty (university) to another, but then they are responsible to stand the tests and examinations for their degrees at the university of their choice and for their ordination. So in America there is no reason why a student might not attend a different seminary during one year, in order to study under an outstanding professor elsewhere; but it is the responsibility of that student to be prepared to pass the examinations for graduation at the seminary of his choice. This may tend to give the Lutheran ministry a better theological education, but the standards for degrees must not be lessened to suit the desires of students.

Dynamic Preaching

It is natural to equate a well-trained ministry with great preaching, but observation compels the conclusion that a man may be well-trained as a pastor and be a poor preacher, and, vice versa, great preachers are not necessarily great pastors. This contradiction ought not exist, but, if we are to be realistic, it must be admitted.

The Lutheran seminaries have produced some great preachers and more are on the way. In the past couple decades, via radio and otherwise, more Lutheran preachers have come to public attention than during many previous years.

However, in spite of the attention given to homiletics in the seminaries, there is much in some Lutheran (as well as other church) pulpits which is provocative of lay criticism, such as hemming and hawing, standing on one foot, trying to get the hands in pockets (in spite of robes), ceaselessly gesturing without reference to the words spoken, close reading of sermons as though they had been written a few hours before, little enthusiasm, less conviction, no evident purpose, little relevance, and little clear communication to the listening congregation. These items are indicative of a lack of adequate training, lack of sufficient time for proper preparation, and perhaps lack of proper understanding of the relevance and urgency of the gospel.

Under the auspices of the Board of Higher Education, ULCA, during the summers of 1956 to 1959 institutes on preaching were held at four different seminaries. Their simple and single purpose was to improve preaching in the Lutheran church by careful study of God's Word, by inquiry into sermonic design, by consideration of problems related to sermonic preparation and delivery, and by frank evaluation of sermons delivered by the participating pastors. After each institute in a formal statement the participating pastors concluded that it had been their most stimulating experience since leaving seminary. Some wives were even amazed at the change in their husbands' preaching. The pastors recognized immediately the extensive effect which better preaching would have on the parish life and program. Here's how the pastors put it: "If such institutes would be available on a sound theological basis, other programs of the church, such as stewardship, evangelism, et cetera, might not be needed." And, "a more living and dynamic presentation of God's Word to our people would accomplish far greater results than all the promotional work presently being done in stewardship, evangelism, et cetera." The pastors were not concerned so much with how Luther or Muhlenberg or Walther or any other great Lutheran leader of the past had spoken, but, rather, with the contemporary question: How shall the living Word be spoken through me to a seeking congregation and a dying world? In other words, the concern was not about past experience and tradition, but, rather, with the present possible experience of the living Christ.

There is no doubt but that dynamic preaching is one great problem facing the churches and the seminaries. Preaching determines attitudes toward the Sacraments as well as the whole program of the whole church. Lutheran seminaries can well afford to point more of their efforts toward dynamic preaching for people who are seeking "the way, and the truth, and the life."

Theology for Laity

In a sense all theology is for the laity, since the students in the seminaries are still laity; but the theology is pointed toward the parish minister. For many years some church leaders have been urging more theological studies for the laity who are not planning to enter the ministry. In the Lutheran church President C. C. Stoughton, of Wittenberg University, has been an ardent spokesman for theology for the laity. The Board of Social Missions of the ULCA, under the influence of the experience in Europe, instituted a series of retreats for laymen in the various professions and occupations in order that laymen and theologians might discuss the Christian implications of the work of laymen. The Higher Education Workshop, held under the auspices of the Board of College Education, ALC, during June, 1961, recommended to the Board of Theological Education of that church that it "make such arrangements as may be necessary or advisable which will provide opportunity for theological studies for such workers in the church other than the ordained clergy, who, being academically qualified, will thereby broaden their understanding of the evangelical message of the church and sharpen their insight of the work and purpose of the church."

A beginning could be made in this matter by having each college arrange with a nearby Lutheran seminary to send an especially capable professor who would conduct at the college, on an evening most convenient to most faculty members, a lecture course with ample time for discussion. The seminaries, on their part, might develop a special summer course or institute for laymen, as did Hamma Divinity School of Wittenberg University in the summer of 1961. College faculty members attending such a summer course might be allowed some financial consideration by their respective colleges, and the church's Board of Higher Education might make a contribution on a per capita basis, as was done for the Hamma course. The Board of College Education, ALC, has already announced and advertised lay schools of theology for the summer of 1962 at Luther Theological Seminary in St. Paul, the Evangelical Lutheran Theological Seminary in Columbus, and California Lutheran College at Thousand Oaks. At Central Lutheran Theological Seminary, under a program initiated by the Central States Synod, there is a program in lay reader training.

Whether held at a college or at a seminary, the courses should be under the direction of a seminary unless the colleges have the personnel qualified to offer the courses. All laity engaged in various phases of church work, especially at a church college, should be encouraged to attend. It may be necessary to arrange for a special type of course to be given to laity without college and professional training on a somewhat lower academic level than would be those courses offered to college professors and other professional laity.

This is one of the most important problems confronting the Christian church and its seminaries. The writer agrees with the statement that "the seminary must take the lead in engaging politicians, economists, sociologists, psychiatrists, artists, writers, and other representative modern men in conversation." But there must be more than a conversation. Too much of lay thought is on the level of an ethical activism, which the Greeks taught and which ethical culturalists of our day delight to proclaim. The seminaries ought to be able to indicate applications and implications of the gospel, the living Word, to all occupations in a way which would be most revealing, enlightening, and compelling, and which would result in a new way of life for many persons. Laymen want to know that the church is interested in the world in which they live. To provide opportunities for laymen to increase their theological knowledge and to understand its implications for the various occupations would pay large dividends in the years ahead both for the individuals concerned and for the church.

Servant or Critic?

There is no question but that the seminary is the servant of the church. Articles of incorporation, policies of relationship, and stated purposes all point to the one conclusion: it is the duty of the seminary to serve the church in the preparation of its ministry.

In the minds of many clergy and laity the seminaries are the intellectual and spiritual centers of the church. This is the place where there is or should be spiritual insight into God's ways with man, past and present, and what man's response to God has been in the past and should be in the present and future.

If this be a relatively correct interpretation of the way in which people look at the seminaries, then seminaries must do more than maintain the traditions of the church and reflect the thought of the past. Seminaries must be concerned with examining the mission and program of the church as it is today. When such studies and observations are made, it may be that seminaries will need to warn the church of lifeless formalism, ecclesiasticism, organizationalism, synodism, institutionalism, self-righteousness, and man-made confusion. In other words, the seminaries must turn critics to keep the church the indwelling of the living Christ.

Such a conclusion assumes that the seminaries are the intellectual center of the church and that the seminaries are the moral conscience of the church. Brown and May in their comprehensive study, *The Education of American Ministers,* pointed out that even in seminaries there is not always the dedicated and committed life and that a major responsibility of seminaries is "the cultivation of the private and corporate devotional life and development of the moral character of the theological student."[7] In other words, the faculties and programs of seminaries must be such as to justify claiming the seminaries to be the intellectual centers and the moral conscience of the church.

This raises the question, Who will criticize the seminaries? Naturally, in the areas of organization, administration, methods of teaching, and content of courses, others can and should speak to the seminaries. In the areas of interpretation of the Word and the development of the spiritual life, the seminaries ought to be

[7] Brown and May, *The Education of American Ministers* (New York: Institute of Social and Religious Research, 1934), Vol. I, p. 155.

able to speak to the church. If that be not the case, then radical changes in the seminaries should take place under the direction of the Word and the experienced intelligence of the church.

Lagging Enrollments

One hundred and fifty years ago Lutherans were seeking to establish seminaries to train men for the ministry; today they are seeking men to be trained in the seminaries. Everywhere denominational leaders are complaining about the need of more men for the ministry. Enrollments in seminaries are not keeping pace with the increases in population, church membership, and college enrollments. The total enrollment in the accredited schools of the American Association of Theological Schools showed a decline in 1960 over 1959, but the enrollments in the fall of 1961 totaled 20,466 as compared with 20,032 in 1960. Canadian schools showed a 10% increase in 1961 over 1960, while in the United States the increase was reported as less than 2%.

The enrollment at Lutheran seminaries is not more encouraging. In the fall of 1951 there were 2,786 registered in the regular seminary courses preparing for the parish ministry; in 1961 the enrollment was 3,180. The increase during the ten-year period was only 394—that is, less than 1% per year. On the other hand, the enrollment in the graduate courses and summer-school sessions of Lutheran seminaries jumped from 268 in 1951 to 1,068 in 1962—that is, an increase of 800 or an average of 80 per year. There is decided interest in positions other than parish ministry.

Why this lag of interest in the pastoral ministry? The American Association of Theological Schools reports that it does not have an answer. Dr. Jesse H. Ziegler, the associate director, indicated the reasons which he assembled from various sources:

1. Competition with recruitment by industry;
2. Questioning regarding relevance of the church and its ministry;

3. Rising costs of theological education for married students;
4. Relative lack of grants comparable to other fields to assist the student without financial resources;
5. Lack of clarity regarding the ministries of clergy and laymen; and
6. Lack of as clear voices speaking appreciatively of church and ministry as those speaking critically.

Here is a distinct challenge both to the seminaries and to the church. In the early 1930's there were not enough vacant parishes for the men graduating from the seminaries. In the 1960's the church has need for more pastors than there are men graduating from the seminaries. Do parents speak of the ministry to their boys? Do Sunday School teachers mention the possibilities of service through the ministry? Are pastors preaching each year on the challenge of the ministry? Are regional synods and national church boards organized with an effective recruiting program? Or have we succumbed to the theory: Do not challenge; do not urge; just allow youth to roam the field of vocational opportunities until they find the one which seems to offer what they think they need? This is a problem for much soul-searching, intelligent study and prayer on the part of Christians everywhere.

CONCLUSION

Theological education has been a vital factor in the growth and development of Lutheran churches in America. It has been in large measure at the center of the Lutheran church, but, it might be said, it has been a dead center to the degree that it has been concerned primarily with problems of the dead past rather than the enlarging future. However, in recent years Lutheran seminaries have been pulsating and struggling with the problems facing the church in the twentieth century. Such a changed point of view is hopeful for the future of the seminaries, of the theologians, and of the church.

III

VENTURING IN HIGHER
EDUCATION FOR THE LAITY

GENERAL BACKGROUND

The church's interest in the field of education forms a vital chapter of American history. In the establishment of academies and colleges the church has been called the prolific mother of schools. Before 1776 eleven colleges were founded, all except one directly or indirectly by religious groups, modeled after the independent colleges of Oxford and Cambridge Universities. By 1865, 182 permanent colleges and universities had been founded, of which some 146 were related to Protestant churches and twelve to the Roman Catholic church. The Baptists, the Methodists, the Presbyterians, and the Congregationalists established most of the schools. The waste in the establishment of educational institutions is seen in a report to the author from one large denomination which said that in 1940 it had 3 universities, 26 colleges, 17 junior colleges, and 149 academies, but that it had closed 174 colleges and 149 academies. Tewksbury reports that, of 516 colleges founded in sixteen states before the close of the Civil War, only 140 remained in 1932, which is to say, 81% were closed.[1]

The establishment of educational institutions is related to the general economic, social, and ecclesiastical conditions. Dr. Abdel Ross Wentz describes rather precisely the various periods of

[1] Donald G. Tewksbury, *op. cit.*

51

American history.[2] Using his descriptive words concerning certain periods, this is what we find: During 1830-1870, "a period of internal discord in the United States, marked by sectionalism and sectarianism," 231 colleges were established, of which 17 were Lutheran, 35 Baptist, 56 Methodist, 32 Presbyterian, 54 other Protestant bodies, and 37 Roman Catholic; during 1870-1910, a period described as one of "big business" with great "expansion" and many new "enterprises," 326 schools were founded, of which 28 were Lutheran, 49 Baptist, 60 Methodist, 40 Presbyterian, 92 other Protestant bodies, and 56 Roman Catholic. It was during this period of expansion that the Protestant church bodies, including the Lutherans, established the largest number of their colleges—269, or about 40% more than in the previous period—but the Roman Catholics established 56 colleges, or 51% more than during the previous period. From 1910 to 1960, a period of "larger units" with increased population and many mergers among Protestant church bodies, 293 colleges were founded, of which 8 were Lutheran, 23 Baptist, 18 Methodist, 8 Presbyterian, 35 other Protestant bodies, and 201 Roman Catholic. It appears that during the last period the Protestant church bodies had reached a point where the number of their colleges was equal to their needs and perhaps ability to support. The total of these figures for the various church groups does not equal the actual number of their existing schools, since a considerable number had been closed or merged with other schools, or their status had been changed.

The facts regarding the founding of Catholic colleges are interesting. In the first two periods the Roman Catholic church established 16% and 17% of the total number, but in the third or last period, 1910-1960, that church founded 201 colleges, or

[2] Cf. A. R. Wentz, *A Basic History of Lutheranism in America* (Philadelphia: The Muhlenberg Press, 1955). It may be questioned whether American history can be divided so easily into periods of forty years each. Nevertheless, they do give an interesting frame of reference for the founding of Lutheran schools.

70% of all the church colleges established during that period. This is accounted for by a change in status for the Catholic population and the special attention paid to education at all levels. Professor John P. Sullivan points out that during the fifty-year period, 1909 to 1959, the total population in the United States increased from 90,492,000 to 175,510,000, or 88.4%, while the Catholic population jumped from 14,220,951 to 35,846,497, or 152%. Sullivan shows, further, that during the same fifty years the number of Catholic colleges and universities grew from 98 to 224, an increase of 128.6%, while the enrollment jumped from 16,040 to 290,578, an increase of 1,711.6%.[3]

During the past twenty years many changes in the status of educational institutions of the various church bodies have been made. Some colleges became universities, some colleges were merged, some junior colleges became four-year colleges, some junior colleges were closed or merged, and some schools gave up their denominational relation. In fact, some schools report themselves under certain circumstances as "private" rather than "Protestant." This is one factor in the difference in figures reported by various agencies. The latest count in 1960 reveals 474 Protestant and 231 Catholic colleges and universities in liberal arts and sciences, excluding professional and technical schools.

As in the previous chapter, lack of space prevents recording desirable historical sketches, which would have revealed the growing venture in higher education as the Lutheran church bodies expanded their work in various states and provinces. Here we shall merely note some interesting episodes and conditions in the establishment of some colleges, without much reference to personalities and synodical groups. There has been added at the end of this book a tabular exhibit of existing colleges listed according to date of founding or opening.

[3] Official Guide to Catholic Educational Institutions, 1960 (sponsored by the National Catholic Welfare Conference, Washington, D. C.), pp. 16-17.

THE FOUNDING OF LUTHERAN COLLEGES[4]

Four-Year Colleges

While individual efforts, such as those by Henry Melchior Muhlenberg and John Christopher Kunze, to establish a Lutheran higher school had failed in the eighteenth century, the first quarter of the nineteenth century tells a different story. Lutherans were developing a denominational consciousness; church leaders as well as educators saw the need for fostering education. The General Synod was organized in 1820. The seminary at Gettysburg was established in 1826. There was no higher school in which students for the ministry could be adequately prepared to take up distinctive theological studies. The Rev. Samuel Simon Schmucker, recognized as "the chief founder of the Seminary," is also called "the founder of the college" at Gettysburg.

Under S. S. Schmucker's leading influence, the board of directors of the seminary voted to establish a Classical School, which name was later changed to Gettysburg Gymnasium. Later he urged "erecting Gettysburg Gymnasium into a college." A group of citizens petitioned the legislature for a charter. The young theologian, invited to address both houses of the legislature, used as his subject "the eminent Character and Services of the Germans in Pennsylvania, and their claims to recognition by the legislature." Finally both houses of the legislature approved the act granting a charter, which gave the name Pennsylvania College of Gettysburg in 1832. Toward the endowment of this college the legislature in 1834, after proper request and expected opposition, made an appropriation of $18,000. With the rapid development of Pennsylvania State College and the consequent confusion of names, it was renamed *Gettysburg College* in the 1920's.

[4] The historical sketches are based upon official statements in catalogues, bulletins, and histories, supplemented by much information, obtained by personal correspondence, which is not otherwise available.

Two graduates of Gettysburg College went to Virginia in 1842 and founded a school near Mt. Tabor Church, about eight miles southwest of Staunton, which was named The Virginia Institute. In 1845 this school was incorporated as The Virginia Collegiate Institute, and two years later was moved to Salem. In 1853 the name was changed to *Roanoke College.*

In the spring of 1844 Ezra Keller, a graduate of the Gettysburg schools, had twenty-four students enrolled in the classics and four in theology at a school in Wooster, Ohio, authorized by the English Lutheran Synod of Ohio in 1842. But the next March 11, 1845, the school was incorporated as *Wittenberg College* with Ezra Keller as the first president, and was located at Springfield. Originally an institution for men only, the college became co-educational in 1874 when nine women were admitted. The school is now organized as a small university with a College of Arts and Sciences, School of Professional Studies, School of Community Education, Divinity School, and Graduate Studies Program in Education. University status was assumed September 1, 1959, and the name changed to *Wittenberg University.*

The schools at Gettysburg could not supply sufficient pastors to care for the needs of the Lutheran church in the states farther west. So the Lutheran Synod of the West (primarily Illinois) organized in 1839, saw the need for an educational institution on its own territory, and took action to establish a Literary and Theological Institute. This was done January, 1847, when an institute was founded at Hillsboro, Illinois, known as Hillsboro College. Financial difficulties and the conviction that a new location was needed for the college caused Hillsboro College to be closed and a new school with a new charter was established in 1852 at Springfield, with the name Illinois State University. Synodical conflicts, students going to war (between the states), and financial difficulties caused the trustees to close the university in 1869. Even with the unhappy experiences of the closing of both Hillsboro College and Illinois State University, the need for an educational institution in Illinois did not disappear. So in 1870 *Carthage College* was established at Carthage, Illinois. During the 1950's the board decided to take the Hillsboro College date of 1847 as their date of origin.

While the Lutherans were venturing in higher education in Illinois, those in Pennsylvania were not idle. In 1848 individuals founded the Allentown Seminary, which name was retained until 1864 when the school was incorporated with full collegiate powers as the Allentown Collegiate Institute and Military Academy. It was in 1867 that the control of the school passed into the hands of a board of trustees, most of whom were members of the Lutheran church. At this time the school was renamed *Muhlenberg College* in honor of Henry Melchior Muhlenberg. Again in 1874 the charter was amended and the control of the college was given to the Evangelical Lutheran Ministerium of Pennsylvania and Adjacent States. The college was for men only until 1957, when coeducation was introduced, although women had studied at the summer sessions for many years previously.

The program of the preparatory school started at Canton, Ohio, in 1830 and moved to Columbus in 1831. It was expanded in 1850 and the school was chartered as *Capital University,* which also included a theological seminary. In 1918 the university was opened to women.

A most complicated story is revealed in the history of *Wartburg College.* Founded in 1852 at Saginaw, Michigan, it was moved the next year to Dubuque, Iowa, where the teacher-training program was soon discontinued. In 1854 concentration was given to the preparatory and theological instruction of men for the ministry. Financial problems caused the school to be moved to St. Sebald, near Strawberry Point, Iowa, in 1857. By 1862 students not studying for the ministry were admitted. In 1868 the college and theological departments were separated when the college was moved to Galena, Illinois. But in 1875 the two schools were recombined at Mendota, Illinois. In 1878 the teacher-training program was revived in the Wartburg Normal College, located at Andrew, Iowa, but moved to Waverly in 1885. In that year the college was moved from Mendota, Illinois, and merged with the normal school at Waverly. Again the college was moved to Clinton, Iowa, in 1894. In 1885 the St. Paul-Luther College was established at Afton, Minnesota, and moved to St. Paul in 1893. The Martin Luther Academy started at Sterling, Nebraska, in 1909 was moved to the Wartburg Normal College at Waverly in 1924. The American Lutheran Church, formed in 1930 through mergers, came to the conclusion that there should be mergers of their midwestern educational institutions. So in 1933 the Eureka Lutheran College, opened at Eureka, South Dakota in 1910, was merged with St. Paul-Luther College. Also in 1933 the Wartburg Normal College was merged with Wartburg College at Clinton, Iowa. But in 1935 Wartburg College was moved from Clinton to Waverly and St. Paul-Luther College was moved to Waverly and merged with Wartburg College. Hebron Junior College, started at Hebron, Nebraska, in 1911 was closed in 1942 and its scholastic records are now on file at Wartburg College.

From the Iowa-Illinois area attention is next drawn to South Carolina, where in 1830 the Lutheran synod had decided to establish a theological seminary and, in connection therewith, a classical academy. Such a school was established at Lexington and was not moved to Newberry until 1856, when *Newberry College* was chartered. The war between the states caused a crisis, and in 1868 the college was moved to Walhalla. However, it was moved back to Newberry in 1877. Summerland College for Women at Batesburg, South Carolina, was founded in 1912 and discontinued in 1930, with any assets and records going to Newberry College.

The beginning of *Susquehanna University* is traced to the establishment of a Missionary Institute at Selinsgrove, Pennsylvania, in

1856 to train men for the ministry. A broader curriculum was soon organized to include the liberal arts and sciences. In 1873 the Missionary Institute pioneered in the field of coeducation by admitting women from the defunct Susquehanna Female College of Selinsgrove. In 1895 the corporate name of Missionary Institute was changed to Susquehanna University, on the basis of its classical or collegiate and theological departments, but the school accepts 1856 as the date of its founding.

The year 1860 is acknowledged as the beginning of two schools. *Augustana College* (Illinois) traces its origin to the founding of a college and seminary in Chicago in 1860 by the Rev. L. P. Esbjörn. This school was moved to Paxton (Illinois) in 1863 and then to Rock Island in 1875.

In that school, founded at Chicago in 1860, *Augustana College* (South Dakota) finds its beginning. After it was moved to Paxton in 1863, apparently the Norwegian supporters separated from the Swedish group and moved their school to Marshall, Wisconsin, in 1869; then to Beloit, Iowa, in 1881; then to Canton, South Dakota, in 1884; and finally to Sioux Falls in 1918. Here in 1889 was founded the Lutheran Normal School which merged with Augustana College in 1918 under the name of Augustana College and Normal School, which was later changed to *Augustana College*.

The Norwegian Evangelical Lutheran Church of America decided to establish a college in 1857, but it was not until 1861 that a building was rented in Decorah, Iowa, for the purpose. However, *Luther College* was started at Halfway Creek, Wisconsin, where the first president, the Rev. Laur. Larsen, could serve as a pastor for immigrants and occupy a vacant parsonage. Apparently this was not satisfactory, for the following autumn, 1862, the college was transferred to Decorah, where it has remained. It started as a college for men and so continued until 1936, when it absorbed the Decorah College for Women.

The Swedes in Minnesota were just as interested in education as were those in Illinois. So in 1862 at Red Wing *Gustavus Adolphus College* was founded as an academy by the pioneer Lutheran pastor, the Rev. Erik Norelius. In 1863 the school was moved to East Union, where it was known as St. Ansgar's Academy. In 1876 the school was moved to St. Peter and renamed Gustavus Adolphus College, in honor of Sweden's famed hero-king. The academy division was discontinued in 1931.

German Lutheran church bodies were also active in extending the boundaries of education in the 1860's in the east-central area. *Northwestern College* was founded at Watertown by the Wisconsin Evangelical Lutheran Synod in 1864, but did not have its academic opening until September, 1865. At first it was named Wisconsin University; then this was changed to Northwestern University and finally to its present name.

The Lutheran Church-Missouri Synod has always been interested in the preparation of teachers for the parochial schools. In 1847 a teachers' seminary was established at Fort Wayne, Indiana, actually to prepare both pastors and teachers. But in 1864 the training of teachers was located at Addison, Illinois. It is known as *Concordia Teachers College* and was moved to its present campus in River Forest, Illinois, in 1913. The program was extended during the years, so that in 1939 it became a four-year teachers' college granting the degree of Bachelor of Science in Education. Since 1938 women have been enrolled, although they attended summer classes since 1932. In 1950, after continual operation for eighty-six years, the high school department was discontinued. Another *Concordia Teachers College* was established at Seward, Nebraska, in 1894 as a preparatory school for the college at Addison, Illinois. This college also expanded rather rapidly, so that in 1939 it operated as a four-year teachers' college.

While Lutherans had already established three colleges and two seminaries in Pennsylvania by 1860, the end was not yet. In 1866

Thiel College was founded as an academy at Phillipsburg, Pennsylvania, primarily because of the influence of the Rev. William A. Passavant on Mr. and Mrs. Louis Thiel, who bequeathed their property for the endowment of an institution to provide Christian education for men and women. In 1870 the school was granted a charter as an institution of collegiate rank and was relocated at Greenville. From 1902 to 1909 the college was temporarily closed.

Augsburg Seminary, which moved from Marshall, Wisconsin, to Minneapolis in 1872, discovered that there was need for a college department in order to have students adequately prepared for theological studies. In 1874 *Augsburg College* was started. In 1900 a high school course was added and discontinued in 1933. Coeducation was introduced in 1921.

St. Olaf's School was founded in 1874 at Northfield, Minnesota, and continued under that name until 1886, when a college department was added. In 1900 the college department of the United Church Seminary, which was located at St. Paul, and in 1917 the college department of Red Wing Seminary, which was located at Red Wing, Minnesota, were merged with St. Olaf.

It was in the 1880's that Lutherans opened a new frontier for education in Kansas. *Bethany College* was started in 1881 as an academy in Bethany Lutheran Church, Lindsborg, Kansas, by the Rev. Carl A. Swenson. It was chartered as a college in 1886 and college classes were started in 1887. The academy was discontinued in 1928.

The Lutherans in the East were not satisfied with the educational situation, so in 1883 at Rochester, New York, the Rochester Lutheran Proseminary was founded by the Rochester Lutheran Conference of the New York Ministerium. In honor of the donor of a site for a campus the name of the school was changed to Wagner Memorial Lutheran College and, more recently, to

Wagner College. In 1918 the college was moved to Staten Island to the noted Cunard property.

While the German Lutherans were active in establishing a school in New York, they were busy in Minnesota also. The first school established by German Lutherans in Minnesota, which remains at this time, was at New Ulm in 1884 with the name of what is now called *Dr. Martin Luther College,* a four-year school devoted specifically to the training of Christian day-school teachers. This college is supported by the Wisconsin Evangelical Lutheran Synod.

While the Swedes were busy in Kansas, the Danes were active in Nebraska. *Dana College* has its roots in Trinity Seminary, founded in 1884. A college was established in 1899 as an institution separate from the seminary, but both occupied the same building.

The General Synod of the Lutheran church was expanding its frontiers in the 1880's and needed men from the great Middle West to minister in their churches. In 1887 that national church body established *Midland College* at Atchison, Kansas, for the purpose of training ministers for the church and teachers for the schools. In 1919 the college was moved to Fremont, Nebraska.

The decade of the 1890's finds the Lutherans still expanding their frontiers. The year 1891 was especially significant with the founding of Chicago Lutheran Seminary (noted in previous chapter), and three colleges in Minnesota, North Carolina, and Texas. Under the auspices of the Northwestern Lutheran College Association, made up of Norwegian Lutherans in the Red River Valley, *Concordia College* came into being at Moorhead, Minnesota, in 1891 as an academy to educate the youth of the pioneers and the large number of immigrant young people. Soon the attendance grew to be over 400. In 1913 a college department was organized and the academy section was disbanded in 1927. Park Region

College, located at nearby Fergus Falls, was merged with Concordia in 1917, due to the merger of church bodies. This Concordia is the only college outside the Lutheran Synodical Conference which uses the name Concordia.

Turning to North Carolina and Tennessee, we find that individuals and congregations there were anxious for a college. Members of the Evangelical Lutheran Tennessee Synod, which included congregations in both Tennessee and North Carolina, founded Lenoir College at Hickory, North Carolina, in 1891, called Lenoir because the campus was given by Captain Walter Lenoir. The name was changed to *Lenoir Rhyne* in 1923 in honor of D. E. Rhyne, who gave the college $150,000.

The Lutheran educational frontier was extended to Texas in 1891, when the Evangelical Lutheran College was founded by the First Evangelical Lutheran Synod of Texas. In 1928 junior college work was started and the name *Texas Lutheran College* was assumed. The school was moved to Seguin in 1912. Trinity College (junior) of Round Rock, Texas, related to the Augustana Lutheran Church, was merged with it in 1929, and likewise Clifton Junior College, affiliated with the Evangelical Lutheran Church, in 1954. The academy division was discontinued in 1932. Senior college work was started in 1948. The college is now supported by the American Lutheran Church, but the Augustana Lutheran Church and the United Lutheran Church also make contributions.

A large number of Swedish people settled in the United States during the latter half of the nineteenth century. Those settling in the New York-New England area wanted a college and established the Upsala Institute of Learning at Brooklyn in 1893, with classes held in old Bethlehem Lutheran Church. This was the beginning of *Upsala College,* which moved to New Orange (now Kenilworth), New Jersey, in 1898 and to East Orange in 1924.

The extreme western frontier of Lutheran higher education in the United States was reached in 1894 when *Pacific Lutheran University* was founded at Parkland, Washington, as an academy. In 1921 it became a junior college, in 1931 a three-year normal school, in 1934 a college of education, in 1941 a college of liberal arts, and in 1960 a university, which was provided for in the original charter. Columbia Lutheran College (1909) and Spokane College (1906) were merged with it about 1920. It is affiliated with the American Lutheran Church and enjoys financial support from the Augustana Lutheran Church.

For a period of thirty years, from 1894 to 1924, no educational institutions which became four-year colleges were established. But in 1924 at Waterloo, Ontario, Canada, *Waterloo College* was established as essentially a child of the seminary, which had been opened in 1911. In 1925 it became affiliated with the University of Western Ontario in an arrangement whereby the university granted the B.A. degree to such students as might be recommended by the college. The *Waterloo Lutheran University* was incorporated in 1960, with Waterloo College becoming the college thereof and the Waterloo Seminary one of its schools. In 1961 it was announced that the Mennonite Brethren College of Winnipeg, Manitoba, had become an affiliated college with the Lutheran university.

Although the history of *Valparaiso University*, Valparaiso, Indiana, traces back to 1859, so far as Lutheranism is concerned it began in 1925, when that university was purchased by the University Lutheran Association, composed of men and women affiliated with the Evangelical Lutheran Synodical Conference of North America. Originally the school was known as Valparaiso Male and Female College. The Civil War brought reverses and a suspension of activities took place from 1869 to 1873, when it was reopened as the Northern Indiana Normal School and Business Institute. The school of law was added in 1879. In 1900 the name was changed to Valparaiso College, and then in 1907 to Valparaiso University.

Another institution which actually began in the second quarter of the twentieth century can trace its history back to the last few years of the eighteenth century, namely, *Hartwick College*. For a number of years Hartwick Seminary (1797) provided for work in high school, beginning college, and seminary. In 1928 the City of Oneonta, New York, located twenty some miles from Hartwick Seminary, with the approval of the Lutheran Synod of New York, achieved the establishment of Hartwick College within its boundaries.

Ventures After 1950

For twenty-five years there was quiet in the Lutheran venture in higher education, but some constructive thinking was going on, which was to prove significant in the third quarter of the twentieth century.

The opening of *Concordia Senior College* at Fort Wayne, Indiana, by The Lutheran Church-Missouri Synod was a unique venture, since it was the only school of its type in American Protestant education in the preparation of men for the ministry. (It appears—although this is not confirmed—that there are 17 of the upper division college type of schools in the Roman Catholic system.) It was authorized in 1947, its plans were approved in 1953, and it was opened in 1957 with a faculty of 23 and a student body of 194 under the presidency of Dr. Martin J. Neeb, who largely masterminded its development. The architecture of the chapel and the arrangement of the campus are among the most distinctive in America.

The establishment of *California Lutheran College* at Thousand Oaks, near Los Angeles, in September, 1961, was another unique

venture with the co-operation of five different Lutheran bodies:
The American Lutheran Church, the Augustana Lutheran Church,
the Evangelical Lutheran Church, the United Evangelical Lutheran
Church, and the United Lutheran Church in America. This college is the direct result of the work of a committee of five executives of Lutheran boards of education who studied the California
situation and printed their report in 1954 in a brochure entitled
"Lutheran Educational Possibilities in California." The California
Lutheran Educational Foundation was organized, with representatives from each of the above-mentioned church bodies. In due
time California Lutheran College was incorporated and later
opened in 1961 with a class of 300 and a faculty of 40, of whom
60% have the earned doctorate. Dr. Orville Dahl is the president
and was the guiding spirit in the development of the college. No
other Lutheran college has ever been started with the support of
five Lutheran bodies and under such significant conditions.

The third venture during this third quarter of the twentieth
century is the establishment by *Carthage College* of a branch college at Kenosha, Wisconsin, in 1962. This college also was the
direct result of a study entitled "Lutheran Educational Possibilities in Wisconsin," published in 1954, at the request of the Synod
of the Northwest. The key sentence in that report reads, "The
State of Wisconsin with an estimated 700,000 Lutherans is the
only state with more than 200,000 Lutherans without a regular
Lutheran liberal arts college, which can be a training center for
Lutheran leadership in church, community and government."

Junior Colleges

Although most of the existing four-year colleges were started
as academies or the equivalent of junior colleges to prepare students for the ministry, they all were developed into four-year
colleges, with the exception of the Concordia Senior College at

Fort Wayne, which is what it was planned to be—a two-year senior college. It is interesting to note that none of the existing junior colleges, most of which were started as academies, was founded prior to 1870. In other words, the Lutheran church ventured into the junior-college field after 1870, which was a period of great expansion and new frontiers in America.

All junior colleges and academies established under the auspices of the Lutheran Synodical Conference, or its constituent bodies, or bodies closely related, had as their purpose the preparation of men for the ministry and teachers for parish schools. The graduates for the ministry go to their respective seminaries. Since 1957 such graduates belonging to the Missouri Synod go to the Concordia Senior College at Fort Wayne for two years and from there to a seminary. Graduates of the Missouri Synod junior colleges, planning to teach in the parochial schools, attend a teachers' college for two years, either at River Forest, Illinois, or Seward, Nebraska. (In the exhibit of colleges at the end of this book all existing junior colleges are noted.)

The Education of Women

The education of women by the Lutheran church, or under Lutheran auspices, in institutions for women only has had an unfortunate history. There is ample evidence that the need for such schools was fully recognized. In the East alone we find "female seminaries" or their equivalent started in Pennsylvania (2), Maryland (3), Virginia (3), North Carolina (4), and South Carolina (1), but none of these exists today. The one shining exception is *Marion College,* started at Marion, Virginia, in 1873, although there appears to be a definite connection with the Wytheville Female Institute started in 1854, which date Marion College could accept as its own.

Mention should be made of Elizabeth College, started at Charlotte, North Carolina, and moved to Salem, Virginia, in 1915. There is evidence that this was a growing institution, but on December 21, 1921, its building was destroyed. Efforts to continue the school as part of Roanoke College or at a new location farther north were of no avail. Here also should be noted the incorporation of The Lutheran College for Women at Washington in 1927. This project was a failure, but after payment of debts the sum of $50,000 which remained was transferred to the supervision of the Board of Education, ULCA. The income is now used to educate young women who wish to prepare for service in the Lutheran Church in America.

Deaconess Schools

In 1910 it was reported that 80% of deaconesses served in the nursing field, but other fields, such as parish education, foreign missions, and social work were opening. In the early 1940's it became evident that the United Lutheran Church desired its deaconesses to have both a college education and special deaconess training for a particular type of work. Under the leadership of Sister Catherine Neuhardt of the Baltimore Training School, with the close co-operation of the executive of the Board of Education, ULCA, a plan was evolved which included three years of college and two years of deaconess training, after which the deaconess received a bachelor's degree. Within the Lutheran Synodical Conference, the Lutheran Deaconess Association has co-operated with Valparaiso University since 1943 in maintaining a deaconess training program, which now includes four years.

In the Lutheran church in North America the training of deaconesses is now definitely on the level of higher education. This is especially seen in the by-laws of the new Lutheran Church in America (X, Boards, B, Item 5), where it says that the Board of College Education and Church Vocations "shall recruit deaconess candidates; conduct training schools. . . ." The whole by-law indicates that this board shall assume the functions of a board of deaconess work. This venture has brought prestige to the professional work of the deaconess and enables her to render her "serving love" in a more intelligent manner to all classes of people.

Without reference to the type of training program they may have today, all existing Lutheran deaconess motherhouses, except one, were established during the period of great expansion and new frontiers in America, as follows: Philadelphia, 1884; Brooklyn, 1885; Omaha, 1887; Minneapolis, 1889; Milwaukee, 1893; Baltimore, 1895; Chicago, 1897; St. Paul, 1902; Brush, Colorado, 1905; and Axtell, Nebraska, 1914.[5]

It is worth noting that the Baltimore Motherhouse was the first to be opened and controlled by a general church body, namely, the General Synod of the Evangelical Lutheran Church.

These historical sketches are a panorama of the Lutheran church in the field of college education for the laity. While at the beginning there was emphasis upon education and training for distinctive church occupations, especially the ministry and teaching in Christian schools, through the years the significance of vocation for the Christian has extended beyond the bounds of the church. So the universities, the colleges, and the training schools are preparing the laity for a life of service anywhere in His Spirit.

THE PRESENT STATUS OF LUTHERAN COLLEGES

In analyzing and summarizing the present status of Lutheran colleges, naturally we must be selective of items which would have the most interest for the prospective hearers and readers of these

[5] See Frederick S. Weiser, *Serving Love, Chapters in the Early History of the Diaconate in American Lutheranism* (Philadelphia: The Board of Deaconess Work, ULCA, 1960), p. 168.

lectures. There are many details which, while important for the total picture, have primary interest only to educators and administrators and will not be discussed.

Figures Tell a Story

In 1940 Wickey and Anderson reported that there were 551 colleges and universities, 189 junior colleges, and 32 colleges and normal schools—a total of 772 church-related colleges.[6] In 1960 the count revealed a total of 712 colleges and universities of liberal arts and sciences, with 481 Protestant and 231 Catholic. This would appear to indicate a decline of 7.7%. Certain denominations, such as the Baptists, Lutherans, Methodists, and Presbyterians, have effected radical changes in the arrangements of their educational institutions.

As for Lutheran schools, *The Lutheran Church Year Book for 1919* lists 39 colleges, 51 academies, and 7 "ladies" colleges and seminaries (or academies) in Canada and the United States. In 1961 the National Lutheran Educational Conference reported 33 universities and colleges and 20 junior colleges. Of the "ladies" schools reported in 1919, only 3 remain today, one being a junior college and two being academies. Of the 51 academies noted in 1919, only 11 remain today, not necessarily as academies, while the other 40 were closed or merged with other schools.

In the context of the American academic community Lutheran colleges and universities are no small factor. They all, as a group, have not achieved such academic significance as to gain special mention, primarily because most of them were founded since 1870 and frequently with linguistic alliances which sometimes prevented a rapid development in accordance with American standards. However, Lutheran schools of higher education are taking a

[6] G. Wickey and R. Anderson, *Christian Higher Education, A Handbook* (Washington, D. C.: Council of Church Boards of Education, 1940). Out of print.

prominent part in American educational affairs in this mid-twentieth century, as will be noted in following pages.

Purpose and Objectives

It is impossible to summarize all the statements of purposes, goals, and objectives of all Lutheran colleges. All Lutheran colleges existing today were founded with a religious motivation: to provide training in the liberal arts and sciences for those preparing for theological studies and the ministry. That motivation is stated today in an expanded and intensified manner, since it is now recognized that all honorable occupations and professions may have a Christian motivation. For example, *Augustana College* (Illinois)

> seeks to transmit the human heritage in the arts and sciences, and encourages full freedom in the search for "whatever things are true, honorable, just, pure, lovely, gracious, excellent, praiseworthy." It seeks to fulfill its vocation to testify to the character and destiny of man manifest in the gospel of Christ and to make known the obligation that rests on every man, especially the educated man, to answer for his life and thought to the Alpha and Omega of all life and truth.

Wittenberg University expresses its fourfold objective in simple, clear-cut phrases:

1. To offer to worthy and qualified students a liberal education under teachers committed to Jesus Christ as divine Lord and Saviour.
2. To prepare students for certain professions or for advanced study in professional or graduate schools.
3. To develop students for intelligent home life, capable church leadership, and conscientious and qualified citizenship.
4. To provide adults with opportunities for continuing education on both undergraduate and graduate levels.

Some colleges are expanding their statements of objectives in such detail that they occupy a whole printed page. The statements of objectives at this mid-twentieth century are superior to those of the nineteenth century in that: (1) they definitely recognize responsibility for the whole student in all his relationships; (2) they give place to the correct conception of Christian vocation in all desirable occupations and professions for which the colleges have a responsibility to give proper education; and (3) they reveal the comprehensive manner in which Lutheran colleges are endeavoring to present an integrated program which affects the student physically, mentally, socially, morally, and spiritually. The critics must admit that Lutheran colleges are clear as to their objectives and that these objectives are comprehensive.

Certain Policies

One of the areas in which church colleges are criticized is that of church relation. Much of it is based upon a lack of knowledge as to legal requirements in certain states, an improper concept of what the church relation should be, and a failure to understand the full import of the relation which does exist.

Christian schools, whatever the academic level, are conceived to be the church in education and part of the church's total program. This is easily recognized on the elementary and secondary levels, but there are varied patterns of ownership and control as pertains to colleges and universities. I have discovered at least seven types of ownership or incorporation involving membership in the corporation. Most of the Lutheran colleges are so incorporated that the membership is elected by regional districts or segments of a national body. Some argue that unless the membership of a corporation of a college is elected by a church body (national or district) that corporation is not Lutheran. Some others would raise the question: Is a group of individual Lutherans, selected to membership in a corporation, less Lutheran because they were not elected by the representatives of a church body? Perhaps the law would require election by a church body to assure proper relationship to that church body, but the author is one who contends that election by a church body does not guarantee the Lutheranism of any individual. If membership in a Lutheran church guarantees the Lutheranism of an individual, then he is Lutheran when he is elected to a corporation, no matter by whom he is elected.

If a college or university claims to be Lutheran, then it ought to accept and welcome consultative and supervisory relationships with the church through its national board of higher education, provided that board employs a staff educated and experienced in the field of higher education. The responsibilities of Lutheran boards of (higher) education vary from that of counselling and co-ordination to that of authoritative recommendation and direction. The powers of such a national board may include a few or all of the following:

(1) to make recommendations to the national convention regarding the establishment, location, and maintenance of educational institutions;

(2) to establish standards or requirements which condition the recognition of a school by the national or regional church body;

(3) to conduct studies, to make surveys, and to counsel with the schools on academic matters, especially as concerns curricular offerings and standards;

(4) to suggest qualified personnel for teaching positions and administrative offices;

(5) to hold conferences of faculty members and administrative officers discussing academic matters and items of mutual interest;

(6) to make financial grants to the schools, supplementing those given by the regional supporting church bodies; and

(7) to encourage where desirable and to approve the arrangements whereby regional bodies of one national church may co-operate in the ownership and maintenance of educational institutions of other church bodies.

Standards and Accreditation

Since higher education in Canada and United States developed without the authority and direction of a national ministry or department of education, as exists in European countries, it is natural that some plan would be evolved whereby educational institutions could and would be evaluated in order to protect the public against false claims and advertising, and to help assure better standards. In Canada each province has a department of education which is concerned primarily with curricula, and there is a National Conference of Canadian Universities (established about 1935) which admits educational institutions into membership depending principally upon their facilities for carrying on an effective educational program. In the United States there is no national accrediting agency, but there are six regional associations, which are the highest accrediting agencies for colleges and universities, since the Association of American Universities withdrew from the accrediting field. These associations are: The Middle States Association of Colleges and Secondary Schools, The North Central Association of Colleges and Secondary Schools, The Northwest Association of Secondary and Higher Schools, The Southern Association of Colleges and Secondary Schools, and The Western College Association. In the United States, in addition to the regional associations, there are state agencies, such as state universities and state boards (departments) of education. The procedure in accrediting generally includes four steps: (1) the establishment of criteria or standards by the agency; (2) the institutional survey by a team of persons supposedly experienced and competent in higher education to determine whether an institution meets the approved standards; (3) report to the official accrediting agency and publication of a list of accredited schools; and (4) periodic reports from the accredited schools to the agency to ascertain whether the school is maintaining the standards. The greatest difference in the accrediting agencies today is the degree of emphasis upon the tangible, quantitative factors, such as credits for graduation, course hours per week, ratio of faculty to students, libraries, academic training of faculty and salaries, and the emphasis upon the intangible factors, such as institutional tone, objectives and their attainment, and outcomes. Of the 33 Lutheran schools reported as four-year or senior colleges, all are accredited except 2 at the time of this writing. Of the 20 schools reported as junior colleges, 14 are accredited.

For the education of women, both in women's colleges and in coeducational institutions, there is the American Association of University Women, which admits into its membership women with degrees from institutions on its approved list. To be so recognized or approved, schools must follow certain criteria which pertain to the education of women. Twelve Lutheran colleges and universities are on this list at present.

Facilities

The facilities of Lutheran colleges have increased greatly during the past forty years. In the Lutheran Year Book for 1919, 39 colleges are listed as having properties valued at about $8,000,000 and endowments at $4,210,000. In 1961 the properties of 33 four-year colleges were valued at $61,202,500—an increase of 665%—and their endowments at $36,495,737—an increase of 766%. The volumes in the libraries jumped during the period 1919 to 1961 from 388,471 to 1,882,000—an increase of 384%.

With the increase in student enrollments beginning in the 1950's, necessity compelled rapid expansion programs in dormitories, student-union buildings, science halls, field houses (formerly known as gymnasiums), administration buildings, and chapels. The facilities of many of our Lutheran colleges compare most favorably with some of the so-called "prestige" colleges.

Curricula

In reaction to the inflexible curricula of the old classical and scientific courses of the nineteenth century, Harvard University developed the free-elective system, which broke down the barriers of rigid requirements. This was copied to a greater or less degree by most American colleges, although Lutheran colleges were less responsive than most colleges of liberal arts and sciences. Then, and closely related, in response to the great commercial, industrial, and scientific developments there followed emphases on occupational and professional subjects. Some colleges added certain courses just to get a few more students. This total situation required a concentration and a distribution in the selection of courses in order to obtain the required number of credits for graduation. In 1945 appeared another noted report from Harvard, entitled *General Education in a Free Society,* which stressed to a large degree, though not absolutely, the opposite of the elective system. This study called for a general education without emphasizing the former liberal education and with no integrating center or principle.[7]

In this third quarter of the twentieth century faculties now realize that there can be no constructive and effective educational program unless there be an integrating principle, and that an education does not consist in studying everything. Great educators knew this long before 1960. Consequently, there is a distinct trend toward self-studies by college faculties, as well as by individuals and groups interested in the liberal arts and sciences. Here Lutheran educators have already made a distinct contribution by the publication of the volume *Christian Faith and the Liberal Arts* in 1960. It is altogether likely that in due time other Lutheran groups, and other Christian educators, will bring forth suggestions for the curricula of Lutheran and other Christian col-

[7] Report of the Harvard Committee, *General Education in a Free Society* (Cambridge: Harvard University Press, 1945).

leges which will have as their chief goal the education of the whole person in accordance with a Christian integrating principle.

Methods of Instruction

In the nineteenth century the catechetical and the lecture methods predominated. In the first part of the twentieth century the lecture and discussion methods were the fashion. Of course, the physical sciences had their laboratories. Concordia Senior College, at Fort Wayne, is making a distinct contribution to educational method by having as its basic concept that "instructional facilities should be specifically geared to the type of work which is to be conducted in them." President Neeb reports that on the basis of this concept they have seven types of instructional facilities: split-level rooms, the "wrap-around" room, the large auditorium-type room, the "bleacher"-style room, the seminar room, the standard or "classical"-style room, and the science-laboratory room. The split-level classroom is a distinct innovation for a college. It is reported that similar designs do exist in the Law School Library at the University of Chicago, the Harvard Graduate School of Business, and Carnegie Institute of Technology. At Concordia 70% of the classes use the split-level rooms, which are requested by students and professors. This type is likely to mark a change in classroom construction. Several Lutheran colleges have speech- and language-laboratory rooms, which are spreading rapidly to all colleges and universities which can afford them.

Extracurricular Activities

The program of extracurricular activities on the average American college campus is quite extensive. At Lutheran colleges these programs include religious groups and activities, student self-government, musical organizations, public speaking, debating and writing contests, departmental clubs, social clubs, recreational sports, and intercollegiate athletics. Intercollegiate activities give many college administrations much concern, especially as regards the high costs, inadequate receipts, and the effect on academic work. Many colleges related to the Catholic Jesuit Order have given up intercollegiate football. Only one Lutheran college, namely, Roanoke, has made this venture, so far as the author has been informed. Most of the extracurricular activities have constructive values. The problem is to restrict the students in their participation so that there may be a real study break.

Even though church colleges were founded with a religious motive, and even though courses in religion are required for graduation, there is continuous discussion of the desirability of a required chapel service. This is true at Lutheran colleges also. It is generally admitted that religion cannot be compelled and that the devotional life can only be developed. The trend is to make attendance at daily chapel services voluntary and to have a required weekly convocation, which may or may not have a religious motive and overtone. Visits to Lutheran colleges and observation of their chapel programs reveal that criticisms generally arise where the leadership of the chapel programs is weak.

In the religious field the most distinctive development at Lutheran colleges in recent years is the student congregation, with a campus pastor. This has become a necessity at several schools because the local community congregation does not have a church auditorium or nave large enough to accommodate both its own membership and the Lutheran students. The college congregation is organized by and for students, who determine its program, under the leadership of the campus pastor. In this development students become "participants" in the life of the congregation rather than merely "attendants" at a church service. Membership of the students in the college congregation does not release them from membership in their home congregations. These college congregations have helped to emphasize the idea that the college is a Christian community. They exist at St. Olaf, Luther (Iowa), and Pacific Lutheran University. Others are giving the plan serious consideration.

Administration

At the beginning of this century the chief administrative officers at Lutheran colleges were the president, the dean, the registrar, and a business officer. In a few Lutheran colleges the president was the chief business officer, even as late as the 1950's. In the 1960's college administration has become rather complicated, primarily because of the bulge of students and the extensive building programs. Instead of the director of public relations or of promotion, today we have the Vice-President in Charge of Development, under whom are such activities as publicity, public relations, alumni relations, fund-raising, and student recruitment. Likewise, some schools call the academic dean the Vice-President (in charge) of Academic Affairs. Then there is a Vice-President in charge of Business and Finance. This officer has responsibilities pertaining to investments, building programs, and construction loans; he frequently assists the president in obtaining big gifts. The office of business manager may be kept and may be concerned with the details of employment, housing, purchasing of supplies, financial records, and general management of the business office.

In the reorganization of the administrative affairs and offices of colleges since 1950 there has been a neglect or an overlooking of the fact that a student is more than an academic and business item on the campus. For more than thirty years the writer has contended that there should be a dean of student life or activities, not including the academic but closely co-ordinated therewith. Student housing is more than a business matter. The social life and organizations of students are quite different from the academic. The religious life and activities are not part of the work of the department of Bible and religion. To neglect the life and activities of students, apart from the academic and financial responsibilities, is a most serious defect in college organization and administration. The officer in charge should be in direct relation to the president and on a parity with the academic, the development, and the financial officers.

This presentation of certain aspects of the present status of Lutheran higher education gives some insight into the progress which has been made and a larger appreciation of the achievements and the problems of these schools.

SOME PROBLEMS AND POSSIBILITIES

What are some of the results of the Lutheran venture in education through its colleges? Have Lutheran educators been able to exert a desirable influence in higher education? Have Lutheran colleges been productive of leadership for church and state? Do Lutheran colleges face insurmountable problems? Are there possibilities for Lutheran higher education's becoming more effective in the American scene? While some of these questions will be given attention, they need extensive consideration by someone or some group of educators so that Lutheran higher education will more than survive. This lecture can only touch some of the issues, with the hope that other persons may be given the opportunity to think the matters through to significant solutions.

Conservative but Constructive and Effective Influence

Lutheran colleges have exerted a conserving and restraining influence, at times when extremes were suggested and were followed by others. Lutheran educators were not swept off their feet by behaviorism, experimentalism, and progressive education, although they did recognize any values which may exist in these trends. The basic values of the liberal arts and sciences have been recognized and maintained. For this reason Lutheran colleges have not added to their programs attractive but superficial side shows.

An education may solve problems of an age without conforming itself to the spirit of the age. Lutheran educators agree with Paul that we are not to be "conformed to this world" but to "be transformed by the renewal" of the mind. Much of modern education has put stress upon being adjusted to the situation; the problem is, rather, to change personalities in order that they may control and change the situation. It is not the spirit of the age, but the Spirit of the Ages to whom we must be adjusted. Many years ago Harry Emerson Fosdick said that it is "not the business of religion to set up adjustments but to produce men and women who are morally maladjusted to their environment and who stand out from it and sit in ethical judgment upon it . . . Our modern culture needs no longer accommodation and harmonizers, but intellectual and moral challengers."[8]

For example, through the generations the question has been asked: Should education teach what to think or how to think? Those who object to indoctrination do so in the fields of morals and religion, but in other fields, such as languages and sciences, they accept indoctrination. Lutherans believe that this generation must accept the truths which the past has brought forth, while at the same time keeping their minds open for possible larger truths in the future.

So in its own quiet way Lutheran higher education has been challenging the isms and the methods which tend to sweep a generation and then pass away. This is one of the greatest achievements which any system of education can accomplish.

[8] *The Christian Century,* November 20, 1935, p. 1481.

The inspiration and the encouragement to persist in maintaining this attitude come from the Word of God, so basic in Lutheran higher education.

Christian Commitment of Faculty

During all of the writer's experience in Lutheran higher education, as well as his other contacts in higher education, the one perennial need, outside of finances, has been deepening the Christian commitment of the faculty and students. Trueblood believes that higher education is one of the "lost provinces" of the Christian church.[9]

In most Lutheran colleges the problem is more difficult than in the seminaries, because faculties and student bodies are not pan-Lutheran. While one may not wish all such faculties and students in colleges to be nothing but Lutheran, as Lars Boe of St. Olaf once admitted, such a condition does present some problems on some occasions.

Without being able to discuss this problem at length, the author's conviction may be summarized in these terms: (1) Lutheran colleges and seminaries are first of all educational institutions, but, being founded directly or indirectly by the Lutheran church, they have a supreme obligation to the Church's God and his Kingdom. (2) Faculty members, all of whom should be Christian, have a prior commitment to Jesus Christ, and have a duty to witness for him through all their activities and human relations. (3) The whole atmosphere of Lutheran colleges, universities, and seminaries must be definitely Christian and partake of the spirit of the Christ. (4) All Lutheran educational institutions, as the church in education, are under obligation to use every desirable means, such as teaching, conferences, counselling,

[9] See Elton Trueblood, *The Company of the Committed* (New York: Harper & Brothers, 1961), p. 11.

group meetings, and even convocations, to present the Christian gospel constantly and continuously in some form to all persons related to the campus community. (5) The institutions should employ outstanding persons to function primarily as chaplains, with a maximum responsibility for worship services, group meetings, and personal counselling. In most institutions, with their present enrollments, this would occupy all the time of the chaplain. In the smaller schools the chaplain could engage in a limited amount of teaching. (6) The presidents of the institutions should be so committed themselves that they will not hesitate to manifest a leadership in this matter and to challenge both faculty and students in regard to their commitment.

Departments of Theology in Colleges and Universities

These institutions have their departments of anthropology, biology, geology, psychology, and sociology. It seems logical and proper to have a department of theology, which is claimed to be the queen of the sciences. By placing the study of theology (as such) only in seminaries, the impression is left that only prospective clergy can and should study theology. With the "rediscovery of the laity," called "the church's frozen assets" by Hendrik Kraemer, the church has the responsibility through its colleges and seminaries to prepare them for the varied ministries in which laity may participate, such as teaching, administration, and other types of service, and also to help them to be intelligent Christians. To fulfill these functions the laity must have an understanding of the Christian faith, as interpreted by the Lutheran church, in a language which modern society can understand, to which society will respond. Organizing the study of Bible and religion, now taught in college departments but sometimes thought of as snap courses suited for Sunday School children, as a department of theology in colleges, the equal of any college department with superior teachers, will catch the imagination of college students and encourage a larger number to elect subjects in such a department. Thus a larger number of the laity in churches and communities will be better trained and equipped to face a changing, even revolutionary, world with their Christian witness in all walks of life.

A few non-Lutheran colleges have had schools or departments of theology, but they functioned as the seminaries of the supporting church group. This would not happen in the Lutheran church because of our seminary program. But some officials of seminaries may object to such a change because of a fear that students might think they know theology before studying it in the seminary. Just as medical students are expected to study certain basic courses in biology, et cetera, before attending the medical school, so all pretheological students should be required to take certain basic courses in religion in college. This procedure would raise the courses in the seminaries to a higher level of professional study. Then too, as already implied, all laity, men and women, should be encouraged to take such studies in college as will make them more intelligent in their Christian beliefs and more capable of bearing a Christian witness in any and all types of work and of human relations.[10]

Christian Leaders for Other Countries

The fall of China to communism and the consequent loss of Christian missionary activities, the crises in Africa, the shocking developments in Cuba, and the rumblings and swayings in South America—all these have awakened American church leaders to a tremendous lack in the educational program for Christian leaders in overseas countries. The future of the Christian church in most

[10] The interest of the laity in theology is manifest in other religions. See F. Dean Lueking, "The Christian Minority in a World of Resurgent Religions," an article in *American Lutheran*, Feb., 1962, pp. 7 ff.

of these countries and continents will be decided during this generation, perhaps during this decade. It is reported that there were only 16 college graduates in the Congo when it became independent on June 30, 1960. Now some Protestant leaders are projecting a "crash program" to train nationals for leadership in the new nations of Africa. For example, it is reported that the Methodist Bishop of Rhodesia has requested the Methodist institutions of higher education in the United States to provide scholarships for at least 50 students. While Christian leaders are being awakened, a news release reports that Russia already has opened its Friendship University to provide leaders for Asia, Africa, and Latin America. On November 17, 1960, that university had an enrollment of 500. The President's Committee on Education Beyond the High School wrote prophetically, "World peace and the survival of mankind may well depend on the way in which we educate the citizens and leaders of tomorrow."

Today there are more than 53,000 students from other nations studying in the United States, enrolled in all types of educational institutions. It is estimated that of the total number two thirds come from Asia, Africa, South America, and Latin America—the countries for which Russia is preparing leaders. Many students from these countries, especially Africa, have a varied educational background; their classification is not easy. Dr. John O. Gross, of the Methodist Board of Education, believes that special planning needs to be made for such students, such as short-term programs, orientation periods, special counselling, and classification centers where the aptitudes and interests of the students could be determined and where the students then could be "assigned to the schools where their needs would be most adequately met."

This is where the church boards of education and boards of world missions should co-operate closely. The church's ministry to non-Lutheran campuses can be of great value to the students who attend the nonchurch schools. In fact, the whole church must feel its responsibility to assist all these boards and agencies in the fulfillment of their tasks by the provision of adequate resources to develop and carry on the necessary programs.

The religious and the political situation in many countries challenges the Christian churches in America for the development of a gigantic educational program. The future of the Christian church is directly related to a Christian leadership in every nation on the face of the earth. The Mormon church has recognized this and has spent $5,000,000 for the establishment of a college in Hawaii. It is reported that this college will primarily serve students from the South Pacific islands and the Orient. Already the Methodists have had conversations with the Congregationalists and the Episcopalians about a Christian college in Hawaii. That new state has been called "the melting pot for many nations of the world." Is there need of a Lutheran school?

To evangelize and to educate the leaders and prospective leaders of the non-Christian nations is a large step toward preventing those nations from succumbing to communism. The problems are many and serious, the solutions are costly, but the challenge to the Lutheran church and its program of higher education is clear.

IV

VENTURING IN
THE CAMPUS MINISTRY

The responsibility of the Lutheran church in the field of higher education does not stop with its own educational institutions; this responsibility continues to nonchurch educational institutions, wherever the church's "roving members," as students have been called, may study. The Lutheran church conceives of the campus ministry as primarily pastoral in nature. Included in the framework of this ministry is Christian education, or the teaching ministry. Such an understanding of the campus ministry justifies its inclusion in a study of Lutheran higher education, especially in light of our definition of education, which includes a commitment and decision. What the secular and state university cannot do, the Lutheran campus ministry does and thereby tries to help the students at non-Lutheran schools to obtain a less incomplete education.

Not all persons and church bodies have agreed on the particular context in which religious work for students should be placed. Through the years in the various denominations it has been conceived of as a form of welfare work, as a part of the missionary outreach, as part of the youth work of the church, as running campus USO centers, and as providing staff to play the role of LSA advisors in a LSA Service Station, as was reported by Dr. Donald Heiges in his State of the Union Message to the 1952 staff conference. In the various church bodies, this ministry has been supported generally either by boards of education or boards of missions.

The significant part which the Lutheran church played in the initiation and development of service to students is briefly but well portrayed by Charles P. Shedd in *The Church Follows Its Students*. This whole ministry of the various denominations was greatly enhanced by the activity of the University Commission of the Council of Church Boards of Education, especially during the years 1930-1948, when Lutheran leadership within the council was effective in giving the work a more definite evangelical emphasis. In 1948 the story of the work of the Lutheran church with its students was told in a book entitled *The Lutheran Church and Its Students*. Written by Mary E. Markley at the request of the Board of Education, ULCA, this volume is the first documented history of any Protestant church body of its work with students in American colleges and universities.

In this chapter the writer shall: (*a*) bring together some of the important factors in the historical development of the campus ministry in the Lutheran church, with certain emphases not fully visible fifteen and twenty-five years ago; (*b*) present certain policies and programs in an all-Lutheran frame of reference; and (*c*) indicate some achievements and emerging problems at this point in the history of the campus ministry of the whole Lutheran church in America.

BEGINNINGS

The Lutheran church, as national church bodies or as regional synods and conferences, did not manifest much interest in its roving members until the turn of the twentieth century, when the enrollment in higher education began to grow rather rapidly and a large number of Lutheran youth were attending nonchurch colleges and universities and also non-Lutheran worship on Sundays. (This is equally true of other denominations.)

Interest of Individuals

Prior to the time when any Lutheran body organized and developed the spiritual care of students in nonchurch educational institutions, individual church members caught the vision of a Christian responsibility. Among the Lutherans it is likely that the first work was started at the University of Iowa, Iowa City, where the First English Lutheran Church was organized in 1855. Students and faculty had a part in developing that parish.

Likewise, at the University of Michigan the presence of Lutheran students and the vision of a Lutheran professor had much to do with the establishment of Trinity Church in Ann Arbor. It was in 1892 that Professor Carl W. Belser, a Lutheran pastor, "teaching the Semitic languages at the University . . . interested himself and others in the establishment of a Lutheran church . . . conducted in the English language, for Lutheran students . . . and such other townspeople who might prefer the English Services."[1] A similar situation existed at State College, Pennsylvania (now called Pennsylvania State University) when the presence of students and the foresight of the Rev. Charles T. Aikens, a neighboring pastor, were responsible for the organization of Grace Lutheran Church in 1898.

Special mention should be made of the insight of the Honorable Frank M. Ritter, Esq., of Philadelphia, who has been judged by one who worked with him for many years as "the outstanding figure, pioneer and promoter of work for Lutheran faculty and students in non-Lutheran schools."[2] Through his efforts the Lutheran Student Work Committee of Philadelphia was organized

[1] Markley, Mary E., *The Lutheran Church and Its Students* (Philadelphia: The Muhlenberg Press, 1948), p. 4.   [2] In a personal letter from Dr. Robert Gearhart.

in 1908, and has continued functioning down through the years in full co-operation with the church officials. For this committee, student work was looked upon as a community responsibility.

In these local parishes were developed programs for students, including student Bible classes, discussion groups, and other types which might be of interest and attractive to students. So it is not exactly correct to say that "the earliest student work in the Lutheran Church was that undertaken by the General Council at Madison, Wisconsin."[3] In all fairness credit must be given to the work done by individuals and parishes before church bodies awakened to their responsibility.

Interest of Church Bodies

It was at the insistence of the Rev. W. K. Frick, pastor of the Redeemer Lutheran Church in Milwaukee, who had several students at the University of Wisconsin, that the Board of Home Missions of the General Council in 1907 called the Rev. H. R. Gold to serve an English Lutheran mission at Madison, with the explicit direction that he give special attention to the Lutheran students at the state university. At its meeting in Minneapolis, September 9-16, 1909, the General Council authorized a Committee on Student Life in non-Lutheran schools to inquire "into the religious conditions of student life in non-Lutheran institutions so far as it applies to the Lutheran Church." This committee created at the University of Minnesota the second student pastorate in 1910 on the territory of the Synod of the Northwest.

In 1911 the Board of Home Missions of the General Synod investigated a situation at the University of Illinois where, it was reported, there were two hundred Lutheran students, most of whom were not going to church at all or were joining "other

[3] Leonard, Evenden, O'Rear, *et al., Survey of Higher Education for the United Lutheran Church in America* (New York: Teachers College, Columbia University, Bureau of Publications, 1929), Vol. III, p. 5.

churches." The first service was held on September 17, 1911, in the university chapel, when a church council of six was elected.

The New York and New England Synod called the Rev. Samuel G. Trexler as the Students' Pastor in 1912. After two years of visiting universities in that territory Dr. Trexler recommended the calling of resident pastors. In 1916 the synod called the Rev. Edwin F. Keever as pastor for the work at Cornell, but he resigned in 1917 when ordered overseas. Then the Rev. William M. Horn was called to that work. His labors were so outstanding that by 1922 a $145,000 church building was dedicated in Ithaca at the gate of the campus.

In the southeastern section of the country work among Lutheran students was started by the Rev. Jacob L. Morgan at Raleigh (North Carolina State College), at Chapel Hill (University of North Carolina), and in Greensboro at the Woman's College (University of North Carolina).

Through such varied beginnings in many quarters, the venture in the campus ministry began to be organized on a national scale.

ORGANIZED DEVELOPMENTS

United Lutheran Church in America

Organized in 1918, through the merger of the General Council, General Synod, and United Synod of the South, this church assigned religious work with students to its Board of Education, which inherited the early accomplishments of the congregations and synods of the merging bodies. Through a department in this board the religious work for students was directed in an extensive and intensive manner until three full-time national secretaries were employed by 1928 and the work became known as outstanding among the denominations in America. The secretaries most responsible for developing this program were: Miss Mary

E. Markley, 1919-1946; the Rev. C. P. Harry, 1921-1946; and Miss Mildred E. Winston, 1928-1946, when the work was transferred to the National Lutheran Council. Miss Winston has continued with the Board of (Higher) Education since 1946, concentrating her attention on church vocations for women and contacting Lutheran women related to the ULCA in any institution of higher learning. She has served in this whole field longer than any other woman in any denomination in America.

Other secretaries who served the ULCA in this field were the Rev. Charles Bauslin, 1918-1930, who gave attention to recruiting men for the ministry. The Rev. Paul H. Krauss, from November, 1919, to December, 1920, did some pioneering in the work among Lutheran students at non-Lutheran schools. Miss Mathilde Peper served on a part-time basis from 1920 to 1928 as assistant secretary for women students. The writer himself has given considerable attention to the campus ministry as executive secretary, Board of Education, ULCA, 1929-1959, and as a member of the Commission on College and University Work, NLC, 1946-1959.

The United Lutheran Church never assumed that it had priority at all institutions. Every effort was made from the beginning in 1919 to have some official agreement or understanding as to which Lutheran pastor should be and would be considered the pastor for students at any one institution. This was true, as the records show, in agreements with officials or representatives of the Augustana Lutheran (Synod) Church, the Evangelical Lutheran Church (formerly called the Norwegian Lutheran Church), and the Lutheran Synod of Missouri, Ohio and Other States (later called The Lutheran Church-Missouri Synod). With the American Lutheran Conference, through its Commission on Student Service, there was agreement as to: (a) geographical areas where each would have supervision and where there would be co-operation of both staffs; (b) holding joint conferences of pastors working with students; (c) guiding and helping the

LSAA; (*d*) printing material of value to pastors and students; and (*e*) developing student work at certain local centers and in certain areas. All these agreements indicated to the ULCA the possibility of a larger co-operation, which was effected in 1946.

The Lutheran Church-Missouri Synod

Student service was started by the Missouri Synod at the University of Wisconsin in 1920, with the Rev. Ad. Haentzschel as the first pastor. Six years later a student chapel, with conjoined parsonage, was erected on a site facing the university campus in Madison. Christian work for students grew rapidly under the direction of the Student Welfare Committee, so that by 1932 there were 74 pastors in 29 states ministering to students. The Rev. R. W. Hahn was elected the first executive secretary in 1940, and still holds that position. In 1944 the name of the committee was changed to Commission on College and University Work. By 1946 it is reported that there were 523 student pastors serving at 727 colleges and universities. In 1961 an official report speaks of 32 full-time and 708 part-time campus pastors. Secretary Hahn began his office in 1940 with a $5,000 budget; in 1961 the budget was almost $100,000 and the Chicago office had a staff of 5. It should be noted that more than 30 geographical districts of the Missouri Synod provide "the hard cash to build chapels and to salary the campus pastors."

American Lutheran Conference

Organized in 1930, the American Lutheran Conference carried on a program of student service from 1938 to 1946 for its member bodies, which included the American Lutheran Church, the Augustana Lutheran Church, the Evangelical Lutheran Church, the Lutheran Free Church, and the United Evangelical Lutheran

Church. The Rev. Fredrik Schiotz, pastor of Trinity Lutheran Church, Moorhead, Minnesota, was called as the executive director, and Miss Hortense C. Hage as his assistant. The Norwegian Lutheran Church had started student service in 1934 on a part-time basis, and from 1935 to 1937 Miss Hage carried on the work until it was taken up by the American Lutheran Conference. The relationships between the staff of this conference and the staff of the board of the ULCA were always very cordial and effective.

National Lutheran Council

At its meeting in December, 1943, the Board of Education, ULCA, took action suggesting the possibility and desirability of the National Lutheran Council's setting up a Department of Student Service for its constituent bodies. This action set in motion steps which led to agreement on the basic principles whereby the United Lutheran Church and the American Lutheran Conference handed over their student work program to the National Lutheran Council on July 1, 1946, when the NLC organized a Commission on Student Service (later renamed Division of College and University Work) and elected the Rev. Morris Wee, pastor of Bethel Lutheran Church (ELC), Madison, Wisconsin, as the first executive secretary, with offices in Chicago. Here was fulfilled an ideal which the board of the ULCA had in mind as early as 1919.

There were two major reservations: (a) that any participating body had the right to visit campuses and counsel with their students concerning church vocations and (b) that full recognition should be given to the Lutheran Student Association of America as a valuable autonomous movement of the church.

When the NLC started its student service in 1946, the national staff consisted of the executive secretary, Dr. Morris Wee; his assistant, Dr. Ruth Wick; two regional secretaries—the Rev.

Oswald Elbert, with an office in Philadelphia, and the Rev. Paul Bierstedt, with an office in Chicago, and an office staff of 3. In that year there were 10 full-time and 16 part-time campus pastors, 298 contact pastors, of whom 14 were in Canada, and 9 full-time counsellors.

For the year 1961 the national staff of the Division of College and University Work of the National Lutheran Council consisted of Dr. A. Henry Hetland, executive secretary; the Rev. Otto Bremer, assistant executive secretary; Miss Burnice Fjellman, program secretary; three field (regional) secretaries—the Rev. Donald Hetzler, the Rev. Gilbert Doan, and the Rev. John Arthur; an office staff of 9 persons. There were 58 campus pastors and about 650 contact pastors. In addition, there were 19 full-time lay workers serving as campus counsellors, 6 full-time seminary interns, and 12 persons listed as part-time assistants.

As for budgets, in 1946-1947 the Student Service Commission of the NLC had a minimum budget of $105,752, while in 1961 the budget was $384,299. To this latter sum should be added the sizable funds expended in local foundations from contributions by individuals, congregations, and constituent units of the participating bodies of the council.

In the development of the campus ministry for the National Lutheran Council, special mention should be made of the work of the Rev. Donald Heiges, who served as executive secretary of the Division of College and University Work from 1950 to 1958. During this period he reinterpreted the campus ministry, exhibited educational and ecclesiastical statesmanship, and effected constructive and extensive developments.

Working behind the scenes in Chicago has been one whose name and service should be here recorded and recognized: Miss Martha Olander has served as office manager and efficient secretary for the campus ministry of both the American Lutheran Conference and the National Lutheran Council since 1938.

Canadian Lutheran Council

With the formation of the Canadian Lutheran Council there was organized a Division of Student Service, which has functioned since 1957 with two regional secretaries and no executive secretary. In 1961 regional secretaries were the Rev. Donald H. Voigts, Saskatoon, Saskatchewan, and the Rev. John A. Vedell, Montreal, Quebec.

HELPS ALONG THE WAY

Foresight and Co-operation of Women

It is remarkable that, while not many Lutheran women attended colleges during the first two decades of the twentieth century, the women of various Lutheran bodies were unusually alert to the need in student service and were prompt in taking appropriate action. During the decade 1910 to 1920 the records indicate that for several years women volunteered to make visits to schools in a program intended "to develop the religious life of college students and to train college women for Christian service." The Lutheran Woman's League of Philadelphia, an autonomous group, which organized in April, 1916, with members from the General Council and the General Synod, had at the start a special interest in Lutheran student work at both Lutheran and non-Lutheran schools. The missionary societies of both the General Synod and the General Council sent representatives to interdenominational summer student conferences in the interests of the Lutheran girls in attendance.

It was through the women's missionary societies of Lutheran bodies that the ministry to students received a great impetus. These societies of both the General Synod and the General Council were especially interested in the welfare of students. In the ULCA the Women's Missionary Society (now called United Lutheran Church Women) from 1920 to 1959 contributed a total sum of $238,219 to the Board of (Higher) Education. They contributed to the salary of a woman secretary until 1946; thereafter the contributions were used as scholarships for young women preparing for missionary work. Contributions from this source have been made to the National Lutheran Council for special work among foreign students.

Another contribution of the society which cannot be estimated in terms of dollars has been the annual student census. Each district synodical society was organized with a student secretary, who obtained the names and addresses of Lutheran students from local congregations wherever the students might be studying. This plan, prepared by Secretary Markley, was initiated during the school year 1919-1920. At first it pertained only to women, but soon included all students. The work has been carried on through the years under the direction of the women secretaries of the Board of Education, ULCA, Miss Markley and Miss Winston. This project stimulated intelligent interest on the part of the women of the church in individual students as well as in the problems of higher education, especially the education of women. In fact, it made realistic the polity of the Lutheran church, namely, the basic position of the local congregation in the whole program of the whole church.

The Lutheran Women's Missionary League of the Missouri Synod had an important place in the development of the campus ministry for that church, "especially in the inauguration of campus work at strategic district-sponsored enterprises by allocating substantial sums of money toward student chapels and student centers." Secretary Hahn reports this was true both nationally and regionally.

The Women's Missionary Federation of the Norwegian Lutheran Church in the 1920's authorized Mrs. Delia Ylvisaker to visit Lutheran schools, but under an agreement in 1924 she was "instructed to extend her activities in Normal Schools of Wisconsin, Minnesota, North and South Dakota, so as to include students of the Augustana Synod and the United Lutheran Church, and to form general Lutheran student groups." This co-operation was valuable and significant.

Co-operation of Boards and Agencies

Boards of home missions were interested especially at centers where the home mission congregation had responsibility for student service. Repeatedly during the past thirty years the author has known of cases where a board of home missions was blind to the church needs of a university community, and pastors engaged in the campus ministry were indifferent to the situation as it pertained to the neighborhood. The Board of American Missions, ULCA, at its September, 1960, meeting faced this problem, with its executive, Dr. Donald H. Houser, giving reasons for a comprehensive study, what the present program is, and the special problems involved. There are prospects that this board and the Division of College and University Work, NLC, will effect a desirable plan whereby more adequate building facilities may be obtained. This is one of the bright prospects for the future.

The Board of Deaconess Work, ULCA, was interested that the claims of the diaconate might be presented to students wherever they might study. Deaconesses as well as the secretaries of the ULCA Board of Education worked together in making such presentations. The youth groups of Lutheran church bodies, such as the Luther Leagues, have been the channels through which some local congregations served the students. When the number of students increased, it was natural that the students wished for their own organizations.

Response of Students

In any situation the response of those with whom one deals is an important factor in future development. Lutheran students in the early years manifested a deep interest by organizing and developing the Lutheran Student Association of America at Toledo, Ohio, in May, 1922. The aims of this association are to promote worship, Bible study, study of the church's activities, service to the local congregation near the campus, contributions to the benevolent work of the church, friendship among Lutheran students, and ecumenical relations with other student groups within the polity of the Lutheran church. Although this association is autonomous and not responsible to the various Lutheran bodies, it has a distinct church consciousness and is very respectful of Lutheran polity. Until September 1, 1961, Lutheran students in Canada participated in the LSAA; since that date these students function in the Lutheran Student Movement in Canada.

For many years the association published a paper, *The American Lutheran Student,* which was later called *The Campus Lutheran,* and then again the name was changed in 1954 to *Frontiers.* Through this medium student opinion is expressed and special programs and projects of the students are strengthened. Besides their offerings to local congregations, the students support special local projects as well as the Lutheran World Federation.

However, with the development and growth of the program in certain ways under the NLC, there was the likelihood that less attention would be given to the LSA on all levels. This Dr. Heiges saw before he left the work in 1958 and in his annual message to the Division of College and University Work staff conference frankly admitted and warned: "In our increasing preoccupation with teaching credit and noncredit courses, inaugurating preaching points, building student centers, expanding foundations, we have been giving less and less attention to the student movements and especially to LSAA in its local, regional, and national manifestations. Furthermore, the development of a *multiphased* campus ministry and program has gradually weakened the once central position of an LSA on the major campuses, and in some places it has entirely disappeared as an identifiable entity. As a result of these factors, and others of a contributory nature, the LSAA stands at a critical moment of its history."

It is little wonder that Dr. Heiges recommended "that the local staff of the Division take a renewed interest in the LSAA and seize every opportunity to strengthen the movement by active participation and loyal support."

Under the campus ministry of the Missouri Synod, local groups assumed the title of Gamma Delta, organized in 1934. In contrast to the Lutheran Student Association, Gamma Delta is a commissioned-sponsored student social organization but is publicized as "The International Association of Lutheran Students." This organization publishes *The Spectator* on a national level. Each region publishes a bulletin, and generally local chapters, of which there are more than 144 in 1961, have their own publications of various types. At this time, according to Secretary Hahn, "student interest in Gamma Delta is growing because the number of chapters is on the increase and there is a greater participation in major regional events, and a number of chapters have reported phenomenal increase in recent years." This does not mean that students are organizationally minded. Continues Dr. Hahn in his personal letter, "While there is an increasing interest in Gamma Delta's activities, there appears to be evidence of a declining interest in organizationalism."

Attitude of Lutheran College Presidents

It is thought that the interest of the synods in their own colleges was the chief reason why some Lutheran college presidents were indifferent to the ministry to students at non-Lutheran schools. To a degree this may be true. But, on the other hand, some college presidents during the early decades of this century were quite active and interested in having their students related to larger student movements; e.g., presidents of these colleges: Carthage, Gettysburg, Muhlenberg, Susquehanna, Wittenberg, and St. Olaf.

VARYING POLICIES

The basic principle on which the work was started and developed was the responsibility of the local congregation(s) to relate students to the life of the congregation(s) and not merely to give them pastoral service, with the district synods or conferences giving the congregational financial assistance for this work. The national board of education was to supplement the financial aid, when necessary.

This policy was explicitly stated by the Board of (Higher) Education, ULCA, in its minutes of May, 1920, in these words: "The Church should be the center of all university student religious work. The religious life of the student should be centered in a Christian congregation. The goal of the student pastor is the cultivation of normal Christian life. This can best be done in a regularly established congregation, ministering the Word and Sacraments and affording fellowship in Worship and Service."

However, this responsibility does not stop with the local congregation; it goes on to the synods and the entire church, as was affirmed by pastors ministering to students in a report submitted to the same board in May, 1924:

"The synod, of which the congregations are a part, is responsible for assisting the congregations in ministering to the students in the community.

"The entire United Lutheran Church has recognized its responsibility for Lutheran students, and through the Board of

Education is prepared to render assistance to synods and congregations in discharging their responsibilities to the students on their territory."

It will be noted that in this statement of policy the responsibilities of the congregations, the synod, and the national church are carefully co-ordinated.

In The Lutheran Church-Missouri Synod there is a somewhat different emphasis with the forming of congregations for the students rather than relying on already established local congregations. In fact, its student work "centers in student congregations housed in campus-side chapels." Its ministry to campuses had and still has a five-point program: "soul conservation, soul reclamation, soul winning, training for Christian service, and Christian impact on the campus." Officials of the Missouri Synod concerned with the campus ministry are now convinced that their emphasis upon worship and the student congregation is the correct one and that as a result they are far ahead of some denominations in work with students. Writing on the subject "Campus Frontiers of Faith" in the May 6, 1961, issue of *Christianity Today,* the Rev. Rudolph F. Norden, the editorial assistant with the Commission on College and University Work of The Lutheran Church-Missouri Synod, says: "Chapels, as both symbols and properly-appointed locales of worship, loom far above social fellowship halls or student centers euphemistically termed 'home away from homes' as starting points for spiritual campus programs. They put communion tables ahead of ping-pong tables. Worship lifts the program, in Richard Celeste's words above a 'punch and cookies affair.' The student congregation, served by a full-time campus pastor, spares the Lutheran collegian of a kind of ecclesiastical schizophrenia. Instead, he is provided with Sunday worship, week-day Bible study, Christian service opportunities, campus evangelism, fellowship and pastoral counseling all in one package. Whatever the student's church-related activity . . . it is under the umbrella of the same campus church." As with the students of the National Lutheran Council, efforts are made to involve students in the whole life of the parish and of the national church.

When the National Lutheran Council assumed responsibility for the campus ministry of its member bodies in 1946, the function of the new division which was established to carry on the work, as stated in the by-laws of the council (Article IX, Section 5), is: "To conserve the faith, to develop the loyalty, and to cultivate the spiritual life of Lutherans in both Lutheran and non-Lutheran educational institutions; to win students and faculty members for Christ and His Church; to discover, to develop, and to direct future leaders of the Church." It is assumed that the human means whereby these objectives will be obtained are the local congregations and any pastors and workers called to assist in the work, the synods, and the national church. In this statement there is strong emphasis upon the spiritual life of the students and the faculty members, making the ministry to the whole campus rather than to the students only. Lutheran and non-Lutheran educational institutions are included. This has always been true in the ULCA, but in the American Lutheran Conference Lutheran schools were excluded. Further, there is the explicit directive "to discover, to develop, and to direct future leaders of the Church"—the vocational emphasis. This vocational interest was manifested as early as 1912 when a committee reported to the annual convention of the New York and New England Synod: "[It is not] simply a question of building a Christian character, but of conservation of wasted forces. Lutheran students at the universities are an immense potential resource. . . . This is the first step towards getting more men for the ministry; the development of power for our Mission and Educational Boards; and the guarantee of a still more efficient and effective laity."

The basic goals of the campus ministry have not been changed by the National Lutheran Council, but there is a definite change in the statement of the means. Prior to 1952, in keeping with the established policy, campus pastors (no matter what their experience, their training, and their ability) were not to preach the Word and administer the Sacraments in student centers at a regular Sunday morning worship service. The division made an exhaustive study of the problem and changed its policy in 1952 (with the permission of the NLC) by allowing for the establishment of preaching points. After proper clearance with church bodies, the foundation at Ann Arbor was the first and the foundation at Lincoln (Nebraska) was the second to be granted the privilege of establishing a preaching point. This change of policy and program was plainly dictated by the logic of events, such as the larger enrollments and the desirability of a complete ministry; otherwise, laymen could have carried on the work.

The most concise statement of the objectives and emphases of the campus ministry today is contained in the annual address of Dr. Heiges to the 1958 DCUW staff conference, which was incorporated in the 1958 report of the DCUW to the National Lutheran Council. That statement is recorded here:

> The Church is at work in the field of higher education in response to her Lord's command to witness to the Gospel "to the end of the earth." Her mission on campus is an integral part of her inclusive mission to make known the Gospel of Christ everywhere and to be of loving service to men and women in all walks of life.
>
> The Church's mission in the colleges and universities must be understood in terms of a ministry *and* a program—a distinction which the Division has made for the past eight years and a distinction which is valid and important; that is to say, the Church's mission includes (*a*) her ministry *to* the campus as well as (*b*) a program *on* campus involving those who live, study, and work there.
>
> With regard to the Church's ministry to the campus, the Divi-

sion has for eight years persistently emphasized (*a*) preaching the Word and administration of the sacraments, (*b*) teaching the Bible, Christian doctrine and ethics, and the history and work of the Church, (*c*) counseling students and members of the faculty, (*d*) calling upon students and members of the faculty, and (*e*) recruiting students and faculty members for service to Christ and His Church.

With regard to a student program, emphasis has been placed upon worship, study, evangelism, service, and recreation. Faculty members have been encouraged to meet periodically to consider their vocation as Christian teachers, to study the relevance of the Christian faith to their particular disciplines, and to develop ways of undergirding the student program.

PROGRAM EMPHASES

In General

From 1920 to 1946 the programs varied at educational institutions, dependent upon circumstances and conditions. They consisted primarily of worship at local congregations, or the student chapel or congregation, Bible study classes, discussion groups, Sunday evening meetings with special speakers followed by discussion and fellowship hours, and area, regional, and national Lutheran student conferences, counselling and recruitment for church vocations. For the information of students and the church, for discussion purposes, and for the spiritual development of students, the national staffs, and others as requested, made many special studies and wrote many folders, pamphlets, and brochures. Including articles for magazines and journals, the number of items runs into the hundreds. Some students with encouragement, and others without encouragement, attended interdenominational conferences, such as the Student Volunteer Movement and meetings organized by the University Commission of the Council of Church Boards of Education, which gave them a larger insight into certain problems and often a deeper appreciation of their own church.

Campus Congregations

Under the direction of the Missouri Synod the emphasis on the student chapel and congregation is strong and primary, with 31 student chapels and 39 student congregations in 1961. Under the NLC the matter of preaching points has been approved and a number established. However, some believe that these preaching points should be given the status of organized campus congregations, with the privilege of serving the entire campus community. This is similar to what happened at Cambridge (Massachusetts) during the 1940's and at Cornell (Ithaca, New York) in the 1920's. Naturally, such steps are dependent upon (*a*) the concentration of Lutheran students and (*b*) adequate guarantees to safeguard the distinctively university-oriented character of such congregations. Under the National Lutheran Council there is no distinct trend toward organizing student congregations as in the Missouri Synod. Perhaps there is needed a variety of congregations, dependent upon the local situation, such as the all-campus, the town-gown in which townspeople predominate, and the gown-town in which the campus people predominate. This may be the approach of the leaders in this field, but it is not always explicitly so stated.

Reports indicate that where there are student or campus congregations the attendance is growing. In fact, Secretary Hahn reported that in some instances the attendance at their student congregations is larger than the number of Missouri Synod students. The NLC officials report also that the attendance at their student congregations is increasing. There is no clear upward trend in the attendance of students at church services in general, but there is "more interest in worship per se and strong desire to have it central to small group meetings."

Campus Centers

The great increase of students and the necessity for adequate facilities to carry on the campus ministry demanded the erection of larger campus centers. Capital expenditures for these centers, including the $550,806 spent before 1947, both actual and authorized for the National Lutheran Council, amount to $5,760,817. The Missouri Synod reports that the total aggregate capital investment "in existing and authorized facilities now approximates $6,000,000."

As a means of helping to obtain larger amounts of financial support from local, area, and regional levels, foundations have been established. A foundation has been defined by the DCUW of the National Lutheran Council as "an agency at a particular school or within a definite geographical area created by the church bodies for the purpose of ministering to students and faculty persons under the supervision of the Division of College and University Work." At present there are only two full-time foundation directors.

Study Courses: Credit and Noncredit

In the summer of 1920 after the author had returned from graduate study at Oxford University, Dr. Howard R. Gold visited me and inquired specifically about possible developments in student work. At that time I strongly recommended a series of courses (noncredit) on a high academic plane dealing with the Bible, ethics, theology of the Lutheran church, apologetics, history of religions, and the philosophy of religion. Although nothing apparently was done with this suggestion directly, nevertheless considerable work was done through various Bible study classes and discussion groups. However, in the fall of 1950 Dr. Heiges, probably without knowledge of the 1920 suggestion, presented to the DCUW a plan whereby a "core-curriculum" of noncredit courses in religion would be presented at such places as the concentration of Lutheran students justified the same. Much opposition developed on the part of some college presidents on the ground that "if this is permitted, a major difference between the Christian school and the state university will disappear." After 1952 the opposition apparently ceased, or at least subsided, and the noncredit course is now an established part of the program under the NLC and the Missouri Synod. Both groups encourage credit courses where allowable and where properly trained personnel are available.

In 1951 Dr. Heiges recommended that credit courses be expanded and "that an Educational Secretary be called to direct the expansion as well as to supervise the noncredit course program." Even prior to 1950 a few credit courses in religion were being taught by Lutheran personnel at the University of North Dakota and Michigan State College. Opposition to the credit courses was more severe than to the noncredit courses, namely, from Lutheran college administrators and officials and from some members of the division on the grounds that such work was "extraneous to our main job in the public institutions of higher learning." After an extended and comprehensive survey of the situation in America as pertains to the existence and possibility of credit courses, made by Dr. George Forell, cosponsored by the Division of College and University Work, National Lutheran Council, and the Commission on College and University Work, The Lutheran Church-Missouri Synod, there was developed a joint program of credit-course teaching. After all eight NLC participating bodies had approved the basic principle, a full-time professorship was established at the University of Iowa on a three-year experimental basis. It proved to be an unusual success, with much favorable publicity for the Lutheran church. The inauguration of similar chairs at other universities is greatly dependent upon the availability of funds from the related regional synods or conferences (districts) and of personnel for such teaching positions.

Special Talent and Interest Groups

This is a day of specialization, even in the campus ministry. From the beginning and through the years efforts have been made to reach all students through a unified program, which had various aspects, such as Bible study, discussion groups, social activities, et cetera. Today an effort is made to serve small special talent and interest groups. The married student with his family constitutes a new category. The graduate student calls for a type of program in which undergraduates may not be much interested, and vice versa.

As early as 1920 home hospitality was accorded to overseas students in New York City. In 1950 Mrs. Lottie Kohls, with many years' experience on the mission field, started work in Berkeley, California. With the financial support of the ULCW, the Augustana LCW, the ELC-WMF, and perhaps others, the service to overseas students on a definitely organized basis has spread to New York City, Boston, Ann Arbor, Minneapolis, and Chicago. More funds are needed to organize and develop the work in Seattle and Washington. It is reported that more than 53,000 overseas students were enrolled in American schools during 1961.

Lutheran Preachers and Speakers

The use of outstanding Lutheran speakers at non-Lutheran events on non-Lutheran campuses was started in 1921 by the Board of Education, ULCA, and has been continued through the years. Besides speaking at university chapel services, convocations, and religious emphasis weeks, these persons often attended meetings of the Lutheran students and thereby enabled the students to become personally acquainted with Lutheran leaders and to obtain a larger view of the Lutheran church.

Many of these speakers received "repeat" invitations from the officials of some of the universities.

Printed Material

Printed material is a valuable instrument in the campus ministry. Besides annual directories, newsletters, and the magazines for students and pastors, the DCUW of the NLC in 1958 published or co-operated in publishing these program materials: *To Walk in Christ, The Living Way,* daily Lenten meditations; *The Coming Messiah,* daily Advent meditations; *The Renewal of the Mind* program series, including "The Christian Doctrine of Man," "The Ecumenical Movement," "The Sacrament of Baptism," "The Sacrament of the Lord's Supper"; *Introduction to the New Testament,* syllabus for noncredit course; and *Faculty Bulletin,* a semi-annual publication mailed to Lutheran faculty.

The CCUW of the Missouri Synod publishes material in rather large quantities. Since 1940 they have distributed 750,000 pieces of literature to their students. Besides the Gamma Delta *Spectator,* they publish the *Lutheran Campus Pastor* monthly during the academic year. Other items published during recent years are: 24 Bible study helps; 76 discussion outlines; 30 tracts on various subjects; "special interest" outlines; and manuals for credit and noncredit courses.

Considering the large printing program of the Board of Higher Education, ULCA, for its student service during 1918-1946, of the American Lutheran Conference during 1938-1946, of the Commission on College and University Work, The Missouri Synod, during 1940-1961, and of the Division of College and University Work, NLC during 1946-1961, it is estimated that up to 5,000,000 pieces of literature were distributed to students and to the churches in the interest of the campus ministry.

An Over-All View

It has been estimated that in 1961 there were about 145,000 Lutheran students in non-Lutheran colleges, universities, and professional schools. Exact figures are not available, since many educational institutions are not allowed by law to obtain the denominational affiliation of students and faculty members. It is further estimated that there are more than 4,000 Lutheran faculty members, administrators, and other officers at non-Lutheran schools. In the same year there were some 1,448 workers, of whom 1,325 were pastors, serving in the whole program of the Lutheran ministry to the campus. The total capital investment in existing and authorized facilities now approximates $12,000,000 in all Lutheran centers. The combined budgets of the two Lutheran groups functioning in the campus ministry amounted in 1961 to $484,299, which did not include sums received by foundations and campus centers from local, area, and regional levels for operating expenses.

What was called "student work" in the first decade of this century is now called "college and university work" or "the campus ministry" for students and faculty members. "Student pastors" are now called "campus or university pastors." The emphasis today is upon a ministry within the whole campus.

ACHIEVEMENTS AND PROBLEMS

Some Achievements

1. The church was awakened to the realization that its roving members (students) are still members and need its ministry. In achieving this, the United Lutheran Church in America was the first to give constant and continuous service to such teaching institutions as normal schools and state teachers' colleges and the first to use women on a full-time basis on a national staff in serving students. Dr. Shedd, in his book *The Church Follows Its Students,* declares, "This action was unique because no other Protestant denomination had thus combined its general religious and missionary interests among students in the leadership of one

person." Shedd further states that other denominations, following the initiative of the Lutherans, appointed secretaries for work among women students, for example, the Protestant Episcopal church and the Northern Baptist Convention.[4]

2. The university is recognized as a great missionary field. Lutheran campus pastors have not neglected this opportunity. No record of what was done through the years is available. The Missouri Synod reports that for 1960 their pastors confirmed 293 students and 4 faculty members. For 1960-1961 the campus and contact pastors of the NLC reported 58 students baptized, 190 students confirmed, and 3 wives of students and 15 children of students baptized.

3. Although the original motive for student work was to follow the student with the church's ministry so as to prevent "falling away" from the church, the vocational motive was also strong. At mid-century the church has found that many students have caught the vision of full-time service in the church and have entered the Lutheran ministry. In its 1960 report to the NLC, the DCUW stated "there were 389 students interested in church occupations, 202 of them in the ministry. The remainder were divided among parish work, college teaching, social welfare, campus work, and missions (but) students here and there are anxious to get into 'frontier' situations—that there is reluctance towards traditional forms of service." This was confirmed by a report that at an ecumenical conference, held in Athens, Ohio, 1958, mission board recruiters "were dismayed by the little interest they found in foreign mission service."

For the Missouri Synod's campus ministry Dr. Reuben Hahn reports that "75% of our current (1961) resident Springfield seminarians are derived from non-Lutheran colleges and universities." Among these, we are told, there are Phi Beta Kappas and two with master's degrees.

[4] C. P. Shedd, *The Church Follows Its Students* (New Haven: Yale University Press, 1938), p. 155.

The Summer Service Project, initiated and conducted through the years by Miss Mildred Winston under the authority of the Board of Higher Education, ULCA, brought together students from various Lutheran bodies for a period of information and instruction, and then placed them in various types of centers, including welfare, recreational and leadership training camps, homes for children, the aging, and the handicapped, hospitals, settlement houses, community centers, and rural and urban parishes. During a twenty-year period this program, participated in by some 1,350 students, coming from some 122 different colleges and universities, "directed the attention of students toward better understanding of the church in its relation to the world community. . . . A study shows that 28% of the persons who were in this program were motivated to enter a church vocation. Many others have used their experience in Summer Service in developing leadership and avocational participation in the church. This program has also sent back to campuses students who vividly have interpreted the Christian faith to fellow students."[5]

Some Problems

1. The lack of a united Lutheran approach in major university centers confronts the Christian conscience of every Lutheran leader. Co-operation with other and all Lutheran bodies was a desire of the Board of Education of the ULCA as early as the 1920's. In spite of what may be called excellent co-operation in some aspects and at some centers, the divided approach at the larger universities is not helpful to the work and does not give a good impression of the Lutheran church.

2. The lack of workers properly trained for their special tasks is a perennial problem for administrators of the ministry to students. Daniel Jenkins, writing on "The Crisis in the University," says: "America has more full-time students' chaplains, whether

[5] Minutes of the United Lutheran Church in America, 1960, pp. 994-995.

appointed by the YMCA, or the churches, in universities of all kinds than any other country in the world. Yet, while a surprising number of these gentlemen show, to the astonished admiration of European visitors, a virtuosity in devising spontaneous entertainments equal to that of the great Danny Kaye himself, their intellectual responsibilities appear to sit very lightly upon their shoulders. With a few shining exceptions their purpose in the university appears to be to run a bigger and better young people's group than in the church back home."[6] The emphasis which the Lutheran campus ministry places on preaching and teaching may remove most of our campus pastors from this condemnation. Nevertheless, the administrators are looking for better-trained and the most capable pastors and leaders for the campus ministry.

Shedd suggests these four qualities for a university pastor: (1) good education and a growing intellectual life; (2) contagious religious life, reasoned faith, dedication to work and happiness in it; (3) attractive personality, with health, humor, love of people, and friendliness; and (4) tact and ability to work with others.[7] These are excellent suggestions, but as the campus ministry has developed there is need also for men, perhaps laymen, with ability for administration and teaching.

3. The town-gown consciousness is an unsolved problem. The question properly arises: To what extent will the ministry to the total campus and the organization of campus chapels and congregations, as now conceived, tend to maintain the separation of town and gown? Are students and faculty sufficiently conscious of their relation to the whole program of the whole church? Are they involved in acts of real Christian service? Do they see their lives related to the life of the neighborhood, not merely of the academic community? While the policy of the 1920's may not be fully applicable to the 1960's, it had a distinctive merit in that it

[6] Daniel Jenkins, "The Crisis in the University," in *Christianity and Crisis*, Vol. IX, p. 166. [7] See C. P. Shedd, *op. cit.*, p. 270.

recognized the unity of the Christian fellowship and discouraged any groupings.

4. Organizations versus committed lives. It was reported above that students are losing interest in a multiplicity of organizations. Is there a tendency in the campus ministry, as well as in the normal congregation, to pile up organizations and then to complain when so few attend the meetings of any one organization? A distinct challenge comes to all pastors and leaders engaged in the campus ministry to concentrate upon obtaining the committed lives of students, faculty, administrators, and all in the academic community. More than thirty years ago John R. Mott told the story of a group's requesting the British War Office for the privilege of doing missionary work among the Indian soldiers during World War I. After several requests and refusals the British Office finally made this proposition: missionary work could be done provided there was no circulation of literature, no preaching, no meetings. The group accepted the offer and performed their missionary work by their daily living. Under every circumstance they endeavored to live Christ and to exhibit that spirit which was in him. Dr. Mott reported that it was the most significant piece of missionary work ever performed. Extensive organization is not necessary for achieving significant results. The challenge on the Lutheran campus and non-Lutheran campus persists for concentration on achieving the committed lives of students and faculty.

V

A CHALLENGE, NOT A VENTURE

Higher education in the Lutheran church is no longer a venture. There is an experience of 136 years in theological education, of 130 years in the education of the laity, of 73 years in the education of the diaconate, and of 55 years in ministering to the non-Lutheran campus. The Lutheran church of today can look upon its program of higher education with commendable pride, fully aware of its weaknesses and needs. Lutheran schools are more firmly established, with larger enrollments, larger endowments, larger facilities, but also with keener competition than ever. Lutheran colleges are growing in quality education and have plans for larger developments. Lutheran seminaries have been strengthened in facilities and have larger financial support. The ministry to the campus is an episode in the history of Lutheran higher education in which the church may have just pride and satisfaction.

In light of the changing times, changing knowledge, changing methods, changing institutions, and changing demands, should the Lutheran church continue its program of higher education? How much farther can and will the Lutheran church go with its program of higher education? Are the continuing crises, national and world, related to a failure in education, secular and religious? Has the church's program of higher education produced such a dynamic leadership as to be an important factor in properly directing the changing times? Have Lutheran schools been established merely to perpetuate the past or to help change the future through changed persons? Does the Lutheran church desire to mold its own youth, as well as other youth, merely so as to be admired by a passing generation, or to fit youth for changing conditions and changing attitudes in human relations and for a permanent society "whose builder and maker is God"?

Although we shall not attempt to answer all of these questions, they must be considered and answered by Lutheran educators and leaders. It is quite proper that attention be given to such questions, with the hope that the Lutheran church, as a whole and in the various bodies, may become so fully awakened and challenged that effective steps may be taken to strengthen the weak spots, to build an unquestionable quality program, and to enlarge the program for the needs of a new day. Whatever else we may say about this age, it is a seeking age—its mind is not fixed— seeking answers to basic questions, seeking something to hold to, seeking someone who will guide. Perhaps a summary view of the major achievements, an indication of some immediate needs, and a brief examination of some problems will assist in giving a reasonable answer as to the prospects for the future. This may be the prologue to the future of Lutheran higher education in America.

SOME ACHIEVEMENTS

If "by their fruits ye shall know them," as Jesus said, then it is worth-while to ascertain and to gather together the assured achievements of the Lutheran venture in higher education, not merely to know the accomplishments but also to appreciate more fully the fruits of the labors of the past so as to build thereon a more enduring future.

1. *Lutheran higher education has promoted and participated, directly or indirectly, in Lutheran unity and co-operation.* In 1910 the National Lutheran Educational Conference was organized, composed at first of presidents of Lutheran seminaries and col-

leges, and secretaries of boards of education. In more recent years executives and pastors related to the campus ministry have been encouraged to attend and participate, as well as Lutheran faculty members. Even as long ago as 1911 Professor V. G. A. Tressler of Hamma Divinity School read a paper on "The Unification of Lutheran Higher Education." Both openly and behind the scenes Lutheran educators have favorably discussed and urged larger Lutheran co-operation and mergers. True educators have an open mind to the truth, "come whence it may and lead whither it will." They see and admit the harmful effects of the separation and isolation of those who acknowledge the same Lord as their Saviour and his Word as their revealed guide. So it is not accidental that more than fifty leaders in the mergers of Lutheran church bodies in 1917, 1918, 1930, 1960, and 1962 were persons who were or are engaged in some phase of Lutheran higher education.

The campus ministry has been an important, though silent, factor in effecting larger Lutheran co-operation. Pastors and leaders came to know and to understand the pastors and leaders of the various Lutheran bodies. Likewise, student leaders in the Lutheran Student Association of America of a generation ago fellowshiped with students from the various Lutheran bodies, worked with them, and understood them. Many of these are now leaders in Lutheran church bodies and are alert to larger Lutheran unity and union.

2. *Lutheran higher education has produced leaders for the church, for education, for the various occupations and professions, and for government.*

Lutheran higher education has a distinct vocational consciousness. The contribution to the ministry of the Lutheran church was noted in the chapter on theological education. Lutheran college faculties and personnel workers are alert to the importance of the students for the ministry on their campuses. No one has yet made a comprehensive and accurate study of the number of men who were definitely influenced for the ministry at Lutheran colleges. Most of such students had planned on the ministry before attending the Lutheran college. In fact, often they attend a Lutheran college because they wish to study for the Lutheran ministry. On the other hand, it is known that each year a considerable number of students at non-Lutheran colleges are directed toward the ministry through the influence of the campus pastors. However, here too we cannot say that the campus pastor and the program for students were the only factors influencing such choices. Quite frequently there are Christian parents, pastors in the home parishes, and Sunday School teachers who sowed seeds of Christian commitment.

In education, graduates of Lutheran colleges have taken significant places in the faculties of American colleges, universities, professional schools, and even non-Lutheran seminaries. For many years Union Seminary in New York and Yale Divinity School were not without a Lutheran representative on their faculties. For several years the theological faculty of the University of Chicago had four Lutherans as members. State and private universities in various parts of the country have appreciated many graduates of Lutheran colleges on their faculties and have advanced some of them to such positions of responsibility as heads of departments and divisions, deanships, and presidencies. Teachers in both secondary and elementary schools in increasing numbers are graduates of Lutheran colleges. There has been a very great increase in the number of Lutheran college graduates in this field, because within the past twenty years Lutheran colleges have given more attention to teacher education. Graduates of Lutheran colleges have been chosen for professorships and deanships on the faculties of law and medical schools.

Towns and cities have their share of Lutheran professional men and women as physicians, surgeons, dentists, and lawyers, who have attended Lutheran colleges. Especially in the Middle West graduates of Lutheran colleges are prominent as state and county officials. Graduates of Lutheran colleges appear to have entered phases of state and federal government to a greater degree in the past twenty-five years than at the beginning of the century.

3. *Lutheran higher education has contributed to the search for and the distribution of knowledge.* This is a quite evident purpose and function of the teacher in the classroom. But the members of our churches know relatively little about the extensive work done by our faculty members in the realm of research and writing. There is a general impression that Lutheran faculty members are not engaged in much writing. This is contrary to the facts. In 1938 the author made a study of the writings produced by faculties of the seminaries and colleges of the United Lutheran Church during a twenty-year period. The results of the study showed that 6 seminaries and 9 colleges reported 83 faculty members producing 199 books, major articles in encyclopedias, and chapters in books. The seminary professors were more productive proportionately than the college professors, with 24 of them writing 76 items, while 59 college professors wrote 123 items. These writings are well distributed in the various fields of theology and the liberal arts and sciences. Some of them are valuable contributions to Biblical commentaries, church history, Christian doctrines, liturgics, Sunday School developments, and catechetical instruction. Some of them are significant contributions to the study of English literature, languages, music, American history, history of education, scientific studies, sociology, and philosophy. Some of them were used as textbooks or required reading in other seminaries and colleges, Lutheran and non-Lutheran.

During what may be called the first century in the history of Lutheran higher education, 1825-1925, the writings were largely prepared for Lutherans only. Perhaps in the period of beginnings, especially with five linguistic backgrounds—Danish, Finnish, German, Norwegian, and Swedish—it was highly necessary that Lutheran scholars should be concerned with strengthening their own church bodies. However, this did not give Lutheran scholars the recognition they deserved.

But during the past thirty years Lutherans in America have been making large contributions in circles far beyond the Lutheran church. This is seen in the recognitions of Lutherans by the World Council of Churches, the National Council of Churches of Christ, USA, the Association of American Colleges, the Council of Protestant Colleges and Universities, and other national and regional church and educational groups. The translations of German and Scandinavian works by American Lutheran scholars have caused non-Lutheran scholars to read and to appreciate Lutheran authors more than ever. The publication of an American edition of Luther's works, as a joint project of Concordia Publishing House and the Muhlenberg Press, under the editorship of H. T. Lehmann and Jaroslav Pelikan, involving the translation of fifty-six volumes by numerous translators, during the period 1955-1970, is a task of tremendous significance for the whole of Protestantism and for at least some of Catholicism. It was two graduates of Gettysburg College and Seminary, Luther A. Weigle and Abdel R. Wentz, who were the only two persons on both commissions concerned with the translation of the Old and New Testaments in the formation of the American Revised Standard Version, with Dr. Weigle as "the prime mover in initiating and carrying through the entire enterprise." Just to mention the names of Lutheran scholars of the past thirty years and their major writings would fill several pages. The productions of Lutheran scholarship during this second century of Lutheran higher education promise to be extensive and constructive.

Too frequently, especially in large universities, undue pressure is exerted on professors to do research and to publish. The impression is left that if a teacher does not publish, he is not productive. While the author has personally encouraged many faculty members in their research and writings, and still does so, he would hasten to say that the primary function of the teacher is to teach. Some teachers neglect this primary obligation for the writing of books. This is not right. The teacher's "chief moral responsibility is toward his students." Lutheran professors have been and are very diligent in attention to their teaching responsibilities. They may not have published so much as have the faculties of some colleges, but they need not be ashamed of the product which comes from their classrooms. Here is where the contribution to knowledge and wisdom is shown in its most effective results.

SOME IMMEDIATE NEEDS

Institutions, like persons, cannot live on the achievements of the past. It is necessary to understand the needs of the present and to endeavor to meet those needs. However, what is considered a present need may disappear with a changed tomorrow. So it is desirable to consider a few of the immediate needs which will help fulfill a long-range program for the changing conditions of the years ahead.

A Philosophy of Lutheran Education

The need for working out a philosophy of education, including higher education, is quite evident from the presentation in the first chapter. No statesmanlike and constructive system of education can be effected without a philosophy which comprehends the whole field of education, including the problems of curriculum, methods, administration, faculty, students, and support. Too frequently even our more outstanding educators find themselves enmeshed with many pressures and ideas striving for first place over the Christian.

This situation calls for the appointment of a special committee, composed of the best minds from the seminaries, colleges, campus ministry, and parishes of all Lutheran bodies. Such a committee should be financially supported by the church boards of education or by grants from foundations, so that at least some of the members could give continuous study and writing for a given period of time until the project is completed. Any statement prepared by this committee could be recommended to the schools (educational leaders) for their consideration and action. The National Lutheran Educational Conference has been asked to assume leadership in such a project.

If an educational program endeavors to develop well-integrated personalities, the program itself ought to be likewise integrated. Perhaps some ineffectiveness in the Lutheran program of higher education is due, not to the students or to the faculties, but to the unintegrated system of education. Such a philosophy of education would not be an ipse dixit which would never be changed but could be passed down to another generation and century. Such a philosophy would need to be re-examined in each generation so as to be certain it is adequate to the needs of the day.

Commission on Research, Planning, and Comity for Lutheran Higher Education

With more than 90% of Lutheranism in America in three large bodies, two of which co-operate in many ways, and with education having so much competition and requiring such large support, the time has come when there ought to be careful studies and agreement before certain next steps are taken. If Lutheranism is what it is supposed to be, and if Lutherans do have a similar philosophy of education, then it would seem both reasonable, logical, and desirable that Lutheran higher education in America in its second century go forward during the second half of the twentieth century in a united front.

It is reported that pressures are being exerted for the establishment of another Lutheran college in Pennsylvania, of a college southwest of Los Angeles (when one has just been opened northwest of the same city), of another seminary in California within fifteen miles of the present one, of a seminary in Texas, and of a college in Georgia. The vision of individuals interested in such projects may be admired, but at this stage in the history of American Lutheranism any new educational institutions ought to have the blessing and encouragement of all Lutheran bodies.

To study these situations and proposals, and to plan for the larger development and expansion of Lutheran higher education, the writer would propose the establishment of a commission on research, planning, and comity in Lutheran higher education. Such a commission should have the approval of the three major Lutheran bodies, which should support it financially. The commission should have authority to make such studies as it may think desirable and as may be requested by responsible boards and bodies, and to make comprehensive reports and suggestions. On the bases of such reports and suggestions the boards and church bodies could take responsible and directive action.

Such a planning commission might have six or nine or even twelve members who are wide-awake and broad-minded educators and churchmen, of whom some should have special ability in research and planning. No hindrances should be placed on the range and depth of research and the suggestions of this commission. The commission might be charged to be fully aware of the socio-cultural conditions and changes in Lutheranism. For a new world with radical changes it should be allowed to suggest a reformation, if not a revolution, in Lutheran higher education.

It is evident that such a planning commission, even though advisory, would help prevent some unwise ventures, would conserve unnecessary expenditures, would prevent unnecessary competition, and would be helpful in the development of a long-range program for all co-operating Lutheran bodies in the field of higher education. Comity committees exist for Lutheran American missions; why not for education?

More Well-Trained Personnel

Charles Malik has been quoted as saying, "Make sure of your teachers and forget about everything else." With the influx of students to American colleges, more teachers with proper training are an absolute need. Many persons with adequate graduate training have been attracted from education to the fields of business and technology. Lutheran college faculties have, on the average, 30% of their members with the earned doctorate, and the faculties of Lutheran seminaries, 40%. Lutheran colleges should have at least 50% of their faculties with the earned doctorate, and seminaries, 60% to 75%.

In light of this total situation the National Lutheran Educational Conference in 1958 adopted a special program of Martin Luther Fellowships, whereby faculty members who wish to complete their graduate studies and obtain the doctorate, and also outstanding seniors in college and seminary who ought to become and wish to become teachers in colleges and seminaries, may be helped financially. During four academic years 1958-1962, this conference has helped 123 men and women to the extent of $161,900, with the financial co-operation of the Lilly Endowment, Inc., and the Lutheran Brotherhood Insurance Society, special gifts from a couple Lutheran boards of education and a number of individuals. These graduate fellows have obtained 26 doctorates and 14 master's degrees. For the training of our future faculty this conference could use $100,000 annually to help guarantee a quality education.

Creative and Dynamic Instruction

It is not our intention to discuss the various teaching methods and to indicate their advantages and disadvantages. It is well known that methods and materials must be relative to the purpose and goal of an educational program. Some instruction should be informing; some instruction should be indoctrinating; and some instruction should be creative.

But there should be more instruction which is creative and dynamic in all subjects, especially in religion. We agree that "the objectives of Lutheran education involve a life of the spirit, a new life within the learner's total being, a basic reorientation and conversion of one's inner being. This would seem to require much more than the instruction in the cold intellectual sense. It calls also for an appeal to the emotions and concern over the application and living out of the instruction."[1] It seems to the writer that this is what Jesus meant when he said: "Teach them to observe all things" and "Be ye doers of the Word."

There are many areas to which Christian instructors can point as needing creative and dynamic living. But at the same time instruction itself must be carried on in a creative and dynamic manner. After examining the theology, psychology, and educational theory of relationships, Jahsmann concludes "that principles and methods of constructive interpersonal and group relations are especially applicable and suitable to the task of Christian nurture and personality development."[2]

It is likely that one point at which criticism may be leveled against some Lutheran educators is their instructional methods.

[1] A. H. Jahsmann, *op. cit.*, p. 72.   [2] *Ibid.*, p. 99.

Often these methods are merely informational and indoctrinational. A great improvement has taken place in this regard during the past twenty-five years, but more needs to be done. Lutherans are not alone in this matter.

Jahsmann considers these characteristics as desirable in the productive activity of a quality group:

1. Its members possess participant roles in the group purposes.
2. Group intelligence is employed in the process of decision-making and also in the final deciding.
3. Activities are keyed to the developmental needs and interests of the group.
4. Much activity is carried on in small face-to-face groups.
5. Communication is full and effectual, also between leaders and group members.
6. Individual integrity is respected, and individual initiative and talent is encouraged.
7. Intrinsic motivation is utilized rather than external devices.
8. Purposes are evaluated regularly.[3]

Many faculty members of Lutheran schools have incorporated to some degree many of these basic principles in their instruction, but Concordia College (senior) at Fort Wayne is the first Lutheran college and, it may be, the first church-related college in America to arrange the classroom facilities so as to help make group activity and participation productive.

Larger Financial Support

Higher education in America, even in the Lutheran church, is big business. The fourteen colleges and ten seminaries of the ULCA increased their assets $50,000,000 in ten years, that is, from $32,383,162 in 1948-1949 to $82,775,526 in 1958-1959. Their expenditures for current funds for 1958-1959 were $16,432,123 as compared to $7,813,797 in 1948-1949. The

[3] *Ibid.*, pp. 92-93.

assets of all Lutheran schools, seminaries, and colleges in 1961 amounted to more than $156,000,000, which represents book value and is very low. While the churches did not contribute all of this total sum, the figures do indicate something of the business transactions of Lutheran schools. But the end is not yet.

The seminaries and colleges of the American Lutheran Church are asking for a special appeal for $20,000,000 in 1963-1964. Wittenberg University alone is asking for $20,000,000 during the decade 1960-1970. The money needed by all Lutheran schools up to 1970 will amount to some $100,000,000, primarily for building purposes. Another $200,000,000 and more could very easily be added to the endowments, the income of which would relieve the needs for funds for current expenditures and faculty salaries, to bring them to the national level.

In the ministry to non-Lutheran campuses, Lutheran church bodies have invested in buildings more than $12,000,000, and more will be needed even in this decade.

So far as the author has been able to ascertain, the Lutheran church has never equaled its zeal for missions with a like zeal for education. A group of Lutheran educators recently put it quite wisely when they said: "The church need not fear that the allegiance of its colleges and schools depends on finances—but their future condition does. Allegiance or commitment cannot be bought, but if the college or school is to carry out the purpose of the church then the church must be ready to support them."[4]

If the Lutheran church is not able to support its schools of higher education, should the church encourage its schools in accepting government support for certain building expenditures and scholarship funds for student aid? This was one of the outstanding questions of the year 1961. The Roman Catholic church came out frankly and forcefully for a share of federal

[4] Proceedings of the Higher Education Workshop, 1961, under the auspices of the Board of College Education, American Lutheran Church.

support for their parochial schools, even at the risk of hindering ample support for the public schools. Protestant groups testifying before Congressional committees gave conflicting opinions on the matter. Protestants in the United States hold definitely to the theory of the separation of church and state, but many of their colleges and universities have accepted federal loans for the construction of dormitories and other income-producing buildings. In Canada outright grants from the government for construction of buildings and even for current purposes are accepted gratefully by both Protestant and Catholic colleges, universities, and even theological seminaries. The Commission on Higher Education of the National Council of Churches in the USA believes that "church-related colleges and universities need to be able to explain *who they are and what they want to do* lest their role and function begin to be defined by others."

Some Lutheran educators do not wish to be entangled in such business matters with the government, with all due respect to all parties concerned. However, the author would raise the question whether we have fully understood the matter of the relation of church and state. Too many statements by Lutherans and others assume the absolute separation of church and state. As Lutherans, we do not believe the state should fulfill the functions of the church, but at the same time we claim that back of the power of the state and of the church lies the power of God. It is interesting that the National Education Association some years ago said: "Separation of Church and State means religious liberty. It does not mean that the government is completely dissociated from religion. . . . The separation of Church and State has never been absolute."[5] Some writers in the Missouri Synod—for example, Dr. A. C. Mueller—advocate a "modified separation." Mayer declares that "Luther's distinction between Church and State was the practical application of the distinction between Law and

[5] *Research Bulletin* (Washington, D. C.), Vol. XXIV, No. 1, p. 7.

Gospel."[6] An elaboration of this principle has been made by Pelikan in an unpublished paper entitled "The Interrelations of Church and State."[7] He thinks of the church as the gospel-proclaiming voice of God and the state as the implementation of God's purpose in his law.

Just as we distinguish but do not separate the Law and the Gospel, so we should distinguish but not separate absolutely the church and the state.

Under such an interpretation the church and its institutions are justified in accepting freedom from property taxes, as well as loans for the erection of buildings not used for religious purposes. In fact, since the state is to some degree responsible for the moral conditions of its citizenry and since Christian education raises the level of moral living, the church would seem justified in encouraging the state to assist individual students to attend Christian colleges and universities with scholarships.

Whatever it may cost the church and the state to support Christian colleges, it will cost the citizens of America more *not* to maintain them. The decline in the moral standards of leaders, the increase in disobedience to the laws of God and man, the failure to understand people and co-operate with one another, the lack of confidence and the increase of deceit, all these and more will bring about a decline in American democracy and an increase in the trend toward a dictatorial communism with its destruction of moral and spiritual values.

This is what William Allen White of Kansas, one of the great newspapermen of America during his day, had in mind when he wrote after a trip to Europe: "Unless those who believe in a Christian civilization are willing to sacrifice of their good, hard earned cash to educate Christian leaders, they will find in a few

[6] F. E. Mayer, *The Religious Bodies of America* (St. Louis: Concordia Publishing House, 1954), p. 135.

[7] Presented at the Educational Conference of The Lutheran Church-Missouri Synod, Milwaukee, Wis., 1950.

generations that their dream has vanished, that tyranny with its hard and fast, ruthless rules of life will be substituted for the good life. . . . It is not a question so much of churches and preachers as it is of colleges that will make leaders who will create a world in which churches can thrive, leaders in all walks of life, in all callings and professions. If American church men fail to support the kind of colleges that turn out Christian leaders, American life under another leadership soon will close the churches."

PROBLEMS AND POSSIBILITIES

Some problems are perennial: solve them today, and they reappear tomorrow in new form. Other problems are relative to special conditions resulting from developments which look toward a larger service or program. To point out a few of these is a concluding responsibility.

Faith and Freedom

At several points in these lectures there has been the implication or direct expression that Lutheran seminaries and colleges are primarily educational institutions and must be supremely concerned with that function, and that at the same time they cannot forget, exclude, or minimize their involvement (not merely relation) with the Lutheran faith, the Lutheran tradition, and the Lutheran program. What freedom does that faith allow?

Lutheran faith accepts Jesus Christ as "the way, and the truth, and the life." The truth of God in Jesus Christ is one, pertains to and includes the whole of reality. All Christian, all Lutheran, teachers seek and have the responsibility and the right to convey the truth at any time, anywhere. Lutheran schools, Lutheran educators, must be liberal in the sense of being open-minded, above provincialism, institutionalism, synodism, and statism, receptive to new truth, with open windows to the whole world of truth, to the end that, by the grace of God, God's image may be restored in man and God's redeeming purpose realized. In this sense Lutheran faith is not contradictory to freedom and upholds intellectual integrity.

There is a distinct sense in which higher education in the church should be the mind of the church, clarifying its functions and program from time to time. Just as the human mind helps the human organism to face conditions, to make choices, and to make decisions, so Lutheran higher education can help the Lutheran church to face the conditions of a changing world and to make decisions as to desirable programs and procedures.[8]

In fact, it is just here that Protestantism is said to be weak. Alfred North Whitehead believes that Protestanism is declining, because "its institutions no longer direct the patterns of life."[9] The schools of the church can suggest new and fresh ways for the church to confront a changing world with the message of salvation. If education comes from the root word *"educere,"* it will lead out, it will stimulate, individuals and organizations to larger visions and creative activity. The spirit of truth still works and wants to work in the lives of people today as in the centuries past. To deny this is to crucify "afresh the Son of God's love" for a lost world.

The schools of the church are personal institutions, not lifeless instruments. They are the servants of the church for the sake of the Kingdom of God, and consequently the church will not allow them to become subservient to any group within or without the church. They should be left free to search for and to witness to the truth of God. The freedom of the church school is the

---

[8] Cf. Nels F. S. Ferre, *Christian Faith and Higher Education* (New York: Abingdon Press, 1954), pp. 236-237.

[9] Alfred N. Whitehead, *Adventures of Ideas* (New York: The Macmillan Company, 1933), p. 205.

Christian freedom for the exercise of administrative responsibility, the intellectual creativity of the faculty, and the moral enthusiasm and intellectual search of students. The educational institutions of the church are under the control only of the Head of the church, who is "the way, and the truth, and the life." This control does not allow license for utterances and acts contrary to revelation and reason, but it does allow the utmost liberty in harmony with God's will.

Upgrading and Expanding the Program

Before our Lutheran programs are expanded, there should be elimination of any fringe subjects started to catch an extra student in the days when the getting of students was a problem. In both colleges and seminaries there should be less fragmentation of curricula and more integration of subjects.

The interest which ministers have manifested in the institutes on preaching, counselling and theology; the need and the demand that the laity be more adequately informed about the basic truths of Lutheran theology; the contributions which the Christian college can make to personnel in the various occupations and professions—all these definitely point toward the need for expanding programs in colleges and seminaries. Before indicating some of the directions or areas for expansion, the writer would state that he does not think all colleges should expand in the same way, nor should all seminaries start competing with one another through certain new programs. Whatever expansion is anticipated should have clearance with the church's boards of college and theological education. For example, at a conference of presidents and academic deans called by the respective boards, it might be agreed as to areas in which the various schools should expand their programs. All too well does the author know the problems which will arise in such conferences, but if the church is to maintain her schools and these schools are to render the desired type and grade of service, then there must be definite co-ordination of and co-operation in programs, especially special programs.

The demand for a *postgraduate school of theology* continues through the years. The United Lutheran Church took the matter so seriously that its constitution was changed so as to allow it to co-operate with other Lutheran bodies in the establishment of such an institution. Institutionalism and sectionalism were the chief hindrances to the project.

Some of the existing seminaries have led graduate programs of various types for many years—for example, Chicago (1894), Philadelphia (1913), Concordia (St. Louis) (1922), and Gettysburg (1928). At Chicago and Concordia some of the graduate students stay in residence until the completion of their studies. In the merger of Augustana, Chicago, Grandview, and Suomi seminaries there is definite provision for a graduate school of theology. Some other seminaries from time to time, upon request of pastors from surrounding territory, have offered some graduate studies.

In light of the total situation, naturally some questions arise: Should all seminaries attempt a graduate program, even for the degree of Master of Sacred Theology? Do all seminaries have the qualified staff and libraries for significant graduate studies? Should Lutheran seminaries attempt the doctoral program? Would Lutheran graduate students prefer to attend a non-Lutheran graduate school? If some Lutheran students were to attend a Lutheran graduate school of theology, would there be sufficient students to justify four such schools, as in Minneapolis, Chicago, St. Louis, and Philadelphia? Do these schools have ample facilities for graduate studies in a doctoral program? Would the church bodies support these programs? Would they be self-supporting? Do the Lutheran bodies related to these seminaries have sufficient confidence in one another so as to be willing to co-operate in a graduate school at one location, where could be gathered an adequate faculty, desirable facilities, and the greatest collection of Lutherans in America?

In the *area of the liberal arts and sciences,* Valparaiso and Wittenberg Universities have graduate programs in a limited number of fields. Pacific Lutheran University has a program in the field of education. Some of the colleges have initiated or are thinking of starting graduate studies in a very limited number of fields.

Here also some questions need to be considered: Will graduate studies change the ultimate goal of the school? Will these graduate programs be self-supporting financially? If not, will the church bodies be asked to increase their grants in order to support these graduate programs? Should all colleges think of upgrading their programs? Are all colleges so fully meeting the requirements and standards for the four-year course that they should think of going beyond? Should the Lutheran colleges in certain areas, like Pennsylvania, the southeastern states, Ohio, Minnesota, Iowa, and the midwestern states confer and try to agree upon the areas in which the respective schools might think of upgrading as well as expanding their programs?

But the term "upgrading" may be interpreted as referring to quality of work, to programs of excellence. It is here that all Lutheran schools, as well as all other church schools, have much to do. Even the large private and state-supported universities do not have quality teachers in all fields of study. No one university is outstanding in all respects. These days of extreme competition do demand that Lutheran colleges and seminaries consider first the quality of their faculties and their programs.

In all thought and discussion of upgrading and expanding the work of a school, consideration must be given to the ultimate purpose of the school. Walter Dill Scott, when president of

Northwestern University, is quoted as saying, "The undergraduate college develops *men*, the professional school develops *specialists*, and the graduate school develops productive *scholars*."

With regard to the growing college population, there is only one answer: The Lutheran church must expand existing colleges and, where Lutheran constituency shows evidence of increasing, new colleges should be established, either as branches of existing institutions or as new institutions.

A Division of Higher Education in a New National Lutheran Council

About 1945 the writer prepared a chart showing a proposed reorganization of the National Lutheran Council. It provided that authority for all NLC work should be received from the Lutheran general bodies and that NLC service would be rendered to Lutheran parishes, groups, and bodies. The six divisions suggested were world missions, American missions, welfare, public relations, parish education, and higher education. In addition, there were some commissions and bureaus. The National Lutheran Council did not include world missions, parish education, and higher education, but did include American missions, welfare, public relations, and campus ministry. Since that time the number of Lutheran bodies has greatly decreased; the possibilities of conflict and misunderstanding have been greatly reduced; and the desirability of a new National Lutheran Council, or its equivalent, with all (or at least the three major) Lutheran bodies members thereof has become evident. Whether the latter is feasible is another question.[10]

During the course of these lectures there were several suggestions which pointed to the necessity and desirability of closer

[10] This paragraph was written before the news release about the conversations between leaders of the Missouri Synod and the National Lutheran Council. It is likely that a new National Lutheran Council will become a reality.

co-operative relations among Lutheran bodies. If the Missouri Synod were to come into the (or a) National Lutheran Council, services such as the following could be included in a division of higher education: (1) the campus ministry, which now experiences embarrassment and sometimes conflict in confronting a college or university campus; (2) a co-operative publicity program for the educational institutions, especially the colleges, so that there would be a united front in presenting Lutheran colleges to the public and the church, and even appearing before governmental committees on matters of mutual interest; (3) a program for obtaining more adequately trained personnel for the seminaries and colleges; (4) a united approach to the training of leaders for the church's program in other continents; (5) the development of a guild of Lutheran scholars from Lutheran and non-Lutheran schools; (6) the preparation of a philosophy of Lutheran education; and (7) the direction of a commission on research, planning, and comity in higher education.

CONCLUSION

Education is "an exciting business," said Edgar M. Carlson, president of Gustavus Adolphus College. This excitement comes not primarily from the dissemination of knowledge but rather from "the expansion of young minds—the growth of human potential." President Carlson goes on to ask, "Who knows what disease will find its cure, or what problem will find its solution, or what need will be met by one student inspired to do his best by an able and understanding teacher?" When both the able teacher and the inquiring student possess the spirit of the Christ, the predictable future is nothing less than the Kingdom of God in the hearts of men wherever Christian education exists.

From a human point of view the future of the Lutheran church is relative to the excellence of its program of education, especially higher education. That program may be excellent in curriculum, in method, in organization, in administration, and in personnel, but above all it must be excellent in spirit—nothing less than the spirit of the Christ who is "the way, and the truth, and the life."

An Italian artist has painted a picture of the "Flight of the Holy Family Into Egypt." Mary is holding the child Jesus while she rides the donkey. Joseph is walking by the side of the animal, but he is looking backward. In the backward look Joseph sees the statue of a heathen goddess with the head broken off lying at the base. There is no couplet to indicate the author's interpretation, but it is commonly interpreted as saying: Joseph is looking backward to a broken age; Mary and Jesus are looking forward to a new world.

In these days of awesome change and development, even of economic, political, and social revolution and scientific miracles, let not the Lutheran church look backward to the "good old days" in its program of higher education; but, rather, let the Lutheran church, with the arms of the various Lutheran bodies in America joined together, look forward to a new world, even the Kingdom of God, in whose coming Lutheran higher education may play a significant role.

Existing Lutheran
Educational Institutions in America

KEY TO ABBREVIATIONS OF CHURCH BODIES

AELC	American Evangelical Lutheran Church
ALC	The American Lutheran Church
AUG	Augustana Lutheran Church
CLC	Church of the Lutheran Confession
ELS	Evangelical Lutheran Synod
LCA	Lutheran Church in America
LFC	Lutheran Free Church
LSC	Lutheran Synodical Conference
MO	The Lutheran Church-Missouri Synod
SUOMI	Finnish Evangelical Lutheran Church (Suomi Synod)
ULCA	United Lutheran Church in America
WISC	Wisconsin Evangelical Lutheran Church

Founded or Opened	Name and Present Location	Supporting Church Body
	SEMINARIES	
1826	Lutheran Theological Seminary, Gettysburg, Pennsylvania	ULCA
1830	Evangelical Lutheran Theological Seminary, Columbus, Ohio	ALC
1830	Lutheran Theological Southern Seminary, Columbia, South Carolina	ULCA
1839	Concordia Seminary, St. Louis, Missouri	MO
1845	Hamma Divinity School, Wittenberg University, Springfield, Ohio	ULCA

Founded or Opened	Name and Present Location	Supporting Church Body
1846	Concordia Theological Seminary, Springfield, Illinois	MO
1854	Wartburg Theological Seminary, Dubuque, Iowa	ALC
1860 (3)	Augustana Theological Seminary, Rock Island, Illinois	AUG
1864	Lutheran Theological Seminary at Philadelphia, Pennsylvania	ULCA
1865	Wisconsin Lutheran Seminary, Thiensville, Wisconsin	WISC
1869	Augsburg Theological Seminary, Minneapolis, Minnesota	LFC
1876	Luther Theological Seminary, St. Paul, Minnesota	ALC
1891 (3)	Chicago Lutheran Theological Seminary, Maywood, Illinois	ULCA
1895	Central Lutheran Theological Seminary, Fremont, Nebraska	ULCA
1896 (1)(3)	Grand View Theological Seminary, Des Moines, Iowa	AELC
1904 (1)(3)	Suomi Lutheran Theological Seminary, Hancock, Michigan	SUOMI
1911	Waterloo Lutheran Seminary, Waterloo, Ontario, Canada	ULCA
1913 (2)	Lutheran Seminary, Saskatoon, Saskatchewan, Canada	ULCA
1920	Northwestern Lutheran Theological Seminary, Minneapolis, Minnesota	ULCA
1939 (2)	Luther Theological Seminary, Saskatoon, Saskatchewan, Canada	ALC
1946	Bethany Seminary, Mankato, Minnesota	ELS
1952	Pacific Lutheran Theological Seminary, Berkeley, California	ULCA

Founded or Opened	*Name and Present Location*	*Supporting Church Body*
1959	Immanuel Lutheran College (Seminary), Mankato, Minnesota	CLC
1962	Lutheran School of Theology, Chicago, Illinois	LCA

Notes: 1. Suomi Lutheran Theological Seminary in 1958 and Grand View Seminary in 1960 affiliated with the Chicago Lutheran Theological Seminary.
2. In 1958 these two schools became a co-operative project but each retained its corporate identity.
3. In 1962 these four schools merged as the Lutheran School of Theology at Chicago, with the merger of their church bodies.

COLLEGES AND UNIVERSITIES (FOUR-YEAR)

1832	Gettysburg College, Gettysburg, Pennsylvania	ULCA
1842	Roanoke College, Salem, Virginia	ULCA
1845	Wittenberg University, Springfield, Ohio	ULCA
1847	Carthage College, Carthage, Illinois	ULCA
1847	Concordia Teachers College, River Forest, Illinois	MO
1848	Muhlenberg College, Allentown, Pennsylvania	ULCA
1850	Capital University, Columbus, Ohio	ALC
1852	Wartburg College, Waverly, Iowa	ALC
1856	Newberry College, Newberry, South Carolina	ULCA
1856	Susquehanna University, Selinsgrove, Pennsylvania	ULCA
1859	Valparaiso University, Valparaiso, Indiana	MO-Related
1860	Augustana College, Rock Island, Illinois	AUG

Founded or Opened	Name and Present Location	Supporting Church Body
1860	Augustana College, Sioux Falls, South Dakota	ALC
1861	Luther College, Decorah, Iowa	ALC
1862	Gustavus Adolphus College, St. Peter, Minnesota	AUG
1865	Northwestern College, Watertown, Wisconsin	WISC
1866	Thiel College, Greenville, Pennsylvania	ULCA
1874	Augsburg College, Minneapolis, Minnesota	LFC
1874	St. Olaf College, Northfield, Minnesota	ALC
1881	Bethany College, Lindsborg, Kansas	AUG
1883	Wagner College, Staten Island, New York	ULCA
1884	Dana College, Blair, Nebraska	ALC
1887	Midland College, Fremont, Nebraska	ULCA
1891	Concordia College, Moorhead, Minnesota	ALC
1891	Lenoir Rhyne College, Hickory, North Carolina	ULCA
1891	Texas Lutheran College, Seguin, Texas	ALC
1893	Upsala College, East Orange, New Jersey	AUG
1894	Concordia Teachers College, Seward, Nebraska	MO
1894	Pacific Lutheran University, Tacoma, Washington	ALC
1924	Waterloo Lutheran University, Waterloo, Ontario, Canada	ULCA
1928	Hartwick College, Oneonta, New York	ULCA
1957	Concordia Senior College, Fort Wayne, Indiana	MO
1961	California Lutheran College, Thousand Oaks, California	ALC-LCA
1962	Carthage College (branch), Kenosha, Wisconsin	ULCA

Founded or Opened	*Name and Present Location*	*Supporting Church Body*

DEACONESS SCHOOLS

(These schools are operated on a college level.)

1884	Philadelphia Training School for Deaconesses	ULCA
1895	Baltimore Training School for Deaconesses	ULCA

COLLEGES (TWO-YEAR)

1873	Marion College, Marion, Virginia	ULCA
1881	Concordia College, Milwaukee, Wisconsin	MO
1881	Concordia Collegiate Institute, Bronxville, New York	MO
1883	Luther College, Wahoo, Nebraska	AUG
1884	St. Paul's College, Concordia, Missouri	MO
1893	Concordia College, St. Paul, Minnesota	MO
1893	St. John's College, Winfield, Kansas	MO
1896	Grand View College, Des Moines, Iowa	AELC
1896	Suomi College, Hancock, Michigan	SUOMI
1903	Waldorf College, Forest City, Iowa	ALC
1905	Concordia College, Portland, Oregon	MO
1906	California Concordia College, Oakland, California	MO
1910	Camrose Lutheran College, Camrose, Alberta, Canada	ALC
1911	Bethany Lutheran College, Mankato, Minnesota	ELS
1921	Concordia College, Edmonton, Alberta, Canada	MO
1922	Alabama Lutheran Academy & College, Selma, Alabama	LSC
1926	Concordia College, Austin, Texas	MO

Founded or Opened	*Name and Present Location*	*Supporting Church Body*
1926	Luther College, Regina, Saskatchewan, Canada	ALC
1959	Immanuel Lutheran College, Mankato, Minnesota	CLC
1959	Milwaukee Lutheran Teachers College, Milwaukee, Wisconsin	WISC

Selected Bibliography

Some of the references are noted for the purpose of background and frame of reference for Lutheran higher education.

Brown, W. A., and May, Mark A., *The Education of American Ministers,* 4 Vols.
New York: Institute of Social and Religious Research, 1934.

Ditmanson, Hong, and Quanbeck, eds., *Christian Faith and the Liberal Arts.*
Minneapolis: Augsburg Publishing House, 1960.

Ferre, Nels F. S., *Christian Faith and Higher Education.*
New York: Abingdon Press, 1954.

Grueningen, John F., ed., *Toward a Christian Philosophy of Education.*
Philadelphia: The Westminster Press, 1957.

Hong, Howard, ed., *Integration in the Christian Liberal Arts College.*
Northfield, Minn.: St. Olaf College Press, 1956.

Jahsmann, A. H., *What's Lutheran in Education? Explorations into Principles and Practices.*
St. Louis: Concordia Publishing House, 1960.

Markley, Mary E., *The Lutheran Church and Its Students.*
Philadelphia: The Muhlenberg Press, 1948.

Medsker, Leland L., *The Junior College: Progress and Prospect.*
New York: McGraw-Hill Book Company, Inc., 1960.

Nickel and Surburg, eds., *Readings in the Lutheran Philosophy of Education.*
River Forest, Ill.: Lutheran Education Association, 1956.

Niebuhr, H. R., Williams, D. D., and Gustafson, J. M., *The Advancement of Theological Education.*
New York: Harper & Brothers, 1957.
Painter, F. V. N., *Luther on Education.*
St. Louis: Concordia Publishing House, 1889.
Redden, J. D., and Ryan, F. A., *A Catholic Philosophy of Education.*
Milwaukee: The Bruce Publishing Co., rev. ed., 1956.
Report of the Harvard Committee, *General Education in a Free Society.*
Cambridge: Harvard University Press, 1945.
Shedd, Charles P., *The Church Follows Its Students.*
New Haven: Yale University Press, 1938.
Snavely, Guy E., *The Church and the Four-Year College.*
New York: Harper & Brothers, 1955.
Tewksbury, D. G., *The Founding of American Colleges and Universities Before the Civil War.*
New York: Columbia University Press, 1932.
Wentz, Abdel R., *A Basic History of Lutheranism in America.*
Philadelphia: The Muhlenberg Press, rev. ed., 1955.

Type used in this book
Body, 11 on 13 and 10 on 11 Garamond
Display, Garamond
Paper: "RRR" Standard White Antique